PROGRESS

The "Our Alberta Heritage" Series

By Jacques Hamilton

Illustrated by Tom Nelson

COMMISSIONED BY CALGARY POWER LTD.

CALGARY, ALBERTA, CANADA

Printed in Canada

INTRODUCTION

Progress is an elusive quality, particularly in a growing Alberta. It is difficult to chronicle the progress of Alberta, for as the very words are put on paper, new events are happening: the progress of today becomes history tomorrow. Northern Alberta is this province's frontier for the 1970s. As the vast resources of the North are developed, the economic and social emphasis in Alberta will shift northward.

In this volume, PROGRESS, we find not so much a chronicle of progress, as a search for a quality — the same quality that appears destined to lead us to an even greater Alberta heritage in the future.

— G. H. Thompson
Chairman of the Board
Calgary Power Ltd.

It is impossible to name them all here, but we would like to express our gratitude to the hundreds of Albertans who so graciously gave their time, their help and their rare records to make this project possible. There are two other people we would like to thank particularly: Mrs. Edith Smith of Calgary and Mrs. Naomi Radford of Edmonton. Without their efforts, these books could never have been completed.

—J. H.

CONTENTS

transportation 1
resource development 25
communication 65
politics and a promise 111

For Condensed Bibliography see end of People book

TRANSPORTATION

"... *without taking the harness off the dogs (we) un-fastened them from the sleds, and pitching them into the water, pelted them with pieces of ice, so that they swam to the other side of the river.*

"*We then got off the edge of the ice ourselves, and found the water took us above the waist, and getting the sleds, loads and all on our shoulders, waded through the rapid, which was about one hundred yards wide, and so reached the left bank.*

"*The wind, which had changed at sunset to N.E. was bitterly cold, so that the plunge into the water felt warm at first, but on re-emerging, we at once stiffened into a mass of ice, for as I found half an hour afterwards, the thermometer stood at −15 degrees.*" (from the records of a trip through the Alberta Rockies in 1858 by Sir James Hector)

* * * *

Travel in Alberta, as recently as the turn of the century, was something a person didn't undertake lightly. The roll of the prairies is deceptively smooth. In fact it is a spine-jarring bed of coulees, sloughs and gopher holes, criss-crossed with steep-banked and treacherous rivers.

In the north, it is thick trees and muskeg. And in the west . . . well, the excerpt above from Sir Hector's journal tells all too well the special challenge of daring the Rockies.

Even the most routine trip in pioneer Alberta could be shattered by tragedy. There is no more horrible illustration of such sudden tragedy than that offered by Rev. James Morrow in his history of the Medicine Hat area.

It was the fall of 1876 and two men, a NWMP constable named Mahoney and an unidentified half-breed freighter, were driving a string of bull-teams west. They came, finally, to the routine obstacle of the Saskatchewan River.

"In crossing the Saskatchewan," Mr. Morrow records "the boat capsized about forty feet from shore. The moment they touched bottom the half-breed instinctively knew he was in quicksand and, as the water was only a little over two feet deep, instead of wading ashore he threw himself flat on it and struck out for land. This undoubtedly saved him.

"However, Mahoney, who was 6 feet, 2 inches in height and weighed over 200 pounds, started to wade out of the river.

"The bottom of the river was no longer sand; it was like muddy glue. Suddenly he sinks in. His feet have disappeared!

"He pulls his foot out and throws himself to the left. The sand comes up over his ankles! He pulls himself out and plunges to the right. Worse! The sand is up to the calf of the Mounted Police boot.

"Then Mahoney recognizes, with unspeakable terror, that he is caught in quicksand and that he has beneath him the fearful medium in which a man can no more walk than a fish can swim. Quicksand to right and left. Quicksand all round him.

"He throws off his load, belt and revolver, and like a ship in distress tries to lighten himself. It is already too late. The sand has climbed above his knees.

"Meantime the breed, like a crazy thing, is running around hunting for a lariat or rope. No use; they are on the other side.

"Poor Mahoney is condemned to that appalling burial, long infallible, implacable, impossible to avoid or hasten, which endures for an hour or two, which seizes a man erect, free, in full health and strength, by the feet and, at every attempt he makes, at every shout he utters, drags him a little deeper, sinking slowly but surely in the bottom of the river bed . . .

"A hand comes to the surface, moves, shakes, disappears, then the current of the Saskatchewan rolls on silently and relentlessly as before Mahoney went to a living death."

A horrible example, true; but one that makes the point.

* * * *

THE FIRST TRAIL . . .

It began at Fort Benton in Montana and snaked northward 200 miles into Canada. Soon it would push west to Fort Macleod, then north to Fort Calgary, and finally it would drive north to the settlements at Red Deer and Edmonton.

It was Alberta's first "highway system", and the first part of it — the 200 miles from Fort Benton — was one of the most important, and most notorious, features of pioneer Alberta.

The name it bore was the "Whoop-Up Trail" because its northern terminal was the infamous whiskey-trading centre of Fort Whoop-Up.

Even today, more than a century later, a visitor to the Lethbridge district can see the deep ruts cut in that trail by loaded ox-carts and, if he has a mind to, he can follow that faint trail southward.

If he does, 66 miles south of Lethbridge at the border town of Coutts, he'll find a cairn and a plaque that gives a valuable clue to the meaning of the Whoop-Up Trail for Albertans.

The plaque reads: "Until the building of the Canadian Pacific Railway across the prairies in 1882 and 1883, the most practicable route to Southern Alberta and Saskatchewan was by the Missouri River to Fort Benton, and thence northward by the Fort Benton (Whoop-Up) trail. This crossed the international border about seven miles west of Coutts. By it came most of the travellers, mail and supplies for the region."

The whiskey traders who pushed that trail north from Benton weren't concerned about anything as noble as the welfare of "travellers, mail and supplies for the region".

But, albeit unwittingly, those traders did perform the people of Alberta a service. The heavy traffic they generated, moving hides one way and trade goods the other, pounded a trail into a road of sorts, and gave Alberta its first real transportation link with the rest of the world.

Mind you, our first "highway" was no route for the impatient. Even under the best of conditions, it took two to three weeks to make the 200 mile trip from Benton to Whoop-Up.

The trail, quite apart from giving access to Alberta, also introduced a new form of transportation — the bull train.

Until the 1860's, the main ways to move goods across the plains were still the canoe, dog-team and pack-horse — all, in terms of capacity, expensive methods of carrying freight.

But now, snorting up from Benton, came the bull train to change all that. Those trains were an impressive sight. The average one would consist of three huge wagons, spaced with stub tongues, and hauled by as many as six to 12 yoke of oxen. Eight to ten of these would travel as a unit, the air above them alive with flies, cracking whips, and enough profanity from the drivers to turn a grown man pale.

In time, the bull trains would be overtaken by fast mule teams, harnessed by sixes and eights, which could cover the distance from Benton to Whoop-Up in half the time of the lumbering oxen (a decided boon for whiskey men trying to keep a jump ahead of the law).

And, still later, the trip would be cut to four to six days by the introduction of the horse-drawn stage coach.

Before the Whoop-Up Trail finally died, with the arrival of the Canadian Pacific line in 1883, it would become a busy route indeed. Even in 1882, the Fort Macleod Gazette recorded that: "There are one hundred teams of all kinds on the road between here and Benton."

* * * *

EAST THEN NORTH . . .

The coming of the CPR killed the Whoop-Up Trail itself, but not its Alberta extension.

The North West Mounted Police had come to Alberta and closed down the whiskey posts in 1874. That done, the force moved west and established a base at Fort Macleod. Soon, however, their patrols had created a road between the fort and the whiskey country around Lethbridge.

Then, as the Mounted Police expanded their network, a road opened between Fort Macleod and Fort Calgary.

The same year the NWMP reached Calgary, 1875, the first crude highway opened between that post and the fur-trading settlement of Edmonton.

Most of the credit for creating the Calgary-Edmonton Trail has to go to pioneer missionary John McDougall — who seems to appear everywhere in the pages of Alberta history.

It was McDougall who cut out the northern half of the route in 1873, to create a cart road between Fort Edmonton and his mission at Morley. The road followed an old Indian trail past the Bear Hills, across the Battle River at Ponoka, over the Red Deer River west of the present city, and turned west at Olds to make a bee-line for Morley.

When the Calgary post was established in 1875, the road was branched at Olds and driven south through Nose Creek and on to the new fort.

By 1883, the road had improved to the point where it was carrying mail and freight and, near the end of the year, stage passengers.

Started by a man in Edmonton, the weekly stage service made the trip between Calgary and Edmonton in five days, with stops at all the settlements in between.

As realization grew that Calgary and Edmonton were probably going to be Alberta's two major communities, efforts to improve the road between them increased.

By 1886, professional surveyors were at work creating the route it would follow into the future.

The surveyor working on the stretch between Red Deer and Edmonton was George P. Roy, and he turned out to be something of a prophet.

"In view of the great traffic and immense travel which some day may be done this way," he wrote in the report of his survey, "my intention was to make the road as straight as the actual direction of the trail between the two extreme points, Red Deer and Edmonton, would allow."

As anyone travelling modern Highway 2 between those points today will agree, Roy was a surveyor who meant what he said.

* * * *

ALBERTA'S FASTEST RIDE . . .

In 1885, even before the surveyors had finished their work on the Calgary-Edmonton Trail, the 200 mile road provided the setting for one of Alberta's outstanding — and probably least-expensive — jobs of riding.

It was the time the Riel rebellion was brewing, and in both Calgary and Edmonton settlers were huddled behind barricades, fearful trouble might spread into Alberta.

In the tension, wild rumors were circulating — and growing wilder by the day. It was critically important that some way be devised to get accurate reports between Calgary and Edmonton so that trouble between white and Indian wouldn't be touched off by accident.

Standing by in both cities were couriers, ready to ride at a moment's notice. In Edmonton, the courier was a man named James Mowatt.

The first detailed reports of the rebellion in the east came in over the telegraph to Edmonton and Mowatt was sent on his way to carry them to Calgary.

Maybe Mowatt was inspired by the urgency of the situation. Or maybe he thought the hills were alive with hostile Indians. No one knows. But whatever the reason, speeding south on horseback, he made the trip that took five days by stage in an amazingly short 36 hours.

And the reward for his historical ride was a slim $26.

* * * *

THE "SQUEALERS" . . .

All the time the route north through Alberta was being built, another route — this one west — was being carved out. Or maybe we should say "screamed out".

"The shriek of a single Red River cart," someone once wrote, "was enough to set tenderfoot visitors writing home: it was an experience of an excruciating kind.

"But when they went out a hundred or two hundred at a time . . . the uproar was beyond imagination. They came like ten thousand devils filing saws, like the Gadarene swine in their frenzy, like the shrieking damned . . ."

Or, as someone only slightly less colorful put it, "The Red River cart brigades never sneaked up on anybody. On a still day you could hear them coming for miles, and see the great cloud of yellow dust they raised.

"And if the buffalo of the plains did finally flee into holes in the ground as the Indians believed — well, it was no wonder."

The Red River cart, invention of the Metis of Manitoba, was as important to the Alberta settler coming from the east as the bull train was to the settler coming from the south.

Physically, the cart wasn't that imposing, but writing of it in the early 1800's, Alexander Henry was quick to spot its virtue:

"Men now go again for meat, with small carts, the wheels of which are one solid piece, sawed off the ends of trees whose diameter is three feet."

By the time the Red River cart pushed into Alberta, it had changed somewhat from the version Alexander Henry described. It had acquired hoops, like a covered wagon, and its wheels had become spoked and stood as tall as a man's head.

But in one way — noise — it hadn't changed at all. The axles were unpeeled poplar or cottonwood logs, and the wheels could not be greased because grease would have collected dust and frozen the hubs to the axles.

Those ugly, noisy carts did an important thing for Alberta. They opened its borders to immigration from the east — and to export to the east.

And if they did sound like "the shrieking damned", ah well, it was only the sound of progress . . .

* * * *

WANNA BUY A REDCLIFF? . . .

From the bumpy beginning of the Whoop-Up Trail, the network of roads in Alberta expanded steadily. By the early years of the 1900's there were paved streets — though not too many of them — and in a matter of a decade or two, Alberta was firmly into the automobile age.

It was so firmly into it, in fact, that it even had a car of its own. Well, it usually came out looking like either a truck or a bus, really, but it was still our own.

"We are the pioneer commercial car builders in western Canada," was the proud claim of Redcliff Motors Co., Ltd.

It was true. Indeed, as history would prove, Redcliff Motors would be western Canada's *only* commercial car builders.

Redcliff, today, is a sleepy little town near Medicine Hat. But for a few years in the 1920's (the exact dates weren't available), it was a thriving industrial community, and Redcliff Motors was its proudest achievement.

The fate of Redcliff Motors — why it went out of business in only a few years — is another of Alberta's historical mysteries. There aren't even any of the company's vehicles left for the historians to ponder.

But, fortunately, an early photographer snapped a couple of pictures of the Redcliff plant, with its trucks lined stiffly out in front of the building. These pictures have survived.

And, thanks to the enterprise of the Redcliff Chamber of Commerce in 1967, Alberta has access to reproductions of one of the company's sales brochures.

From the brochure we can obtain a wealth of technical specifications for their handsome vehicles, and discover that they were quite reasonably priced (by today's standards, at least). A 12-passenger bus, for example, cost only $4,500.

Most importantly, though, we find in the brochure a rare statement of the philosophy that was beginning to reach transportation-conscious Albertans of the day.

"Modern transportation without railroads would be a long stretch of the imagination," the brochure explains. "The common carriers have become absolutely essential to life. Modern industrialism is intimately related to transportation, and a study of transportation has developed many economies in handling materials.

"Yet the small manufacturer, the jobber, and the merchant, to whom economies are surely important, rely on the plodding horse to move their goods."

Time would soon see the manufacturer, jobber and merchant switch to trucks. But time would also dictate that it would be too late for Alberta's pioneering Redcliff Motors to supply those trucks.

* * * *

ALL THIS AND THE MINNOW TOO . . .

If there's anything one wouldn't expect to see sticking out of the prairies of Alberta it's the funnel of a steamboat.

But in the Alberta of the 1880's, that is exactly what was sticking out of our prairies.

Alex Johnson, president of the Lethbridge and District Historical Society, sums up the story in his preface to the book Boats and Barges on the Belly:

"From the beginning, the commerce of Canada moved along her rivers — starting with the epic canoe journeys of the voyageurs, who penetrated the length and breadth of the land.

"Southward, following the invention of the steamboat in 1807, the Mississippi, the Ohio, the Missouri and their tributaries blossomed with side and stern-wheelers that each year carried millions of tons of cargo. By 1873, steamboats had reached the Saskatchewan.

"Thus, in 1883, it was natural to think of steamboats and barges when coal from the Belly bluffs had to be moved to Medicine Hat.

Unfortunately, little was known of the variable flow of the Belly and South Saskatchewan Rivers and no one appreciated how dependent the flow was on snow melt in the mountains. From the outset, the use of steamers on the rivers of southern Alberta was doomed to failure."

There were three of them — all built in Alberta of wood from the Porcupine Hills.

The first, the Baroness, was 173 feet long, a stern-wheeler. She was launched at Coal Banks on July 2, 1883, and floated down to Medicine Hat where she was fitted with her machinery.

The second was the Alberta, also a stern-wheeler, and 100 feet long. She went in the water in 1884.

The third was the Minnow, more tug than steamer. Only 73 feet long and 10 feet wide, she started life as a stern-wheeler but was later converted to propeller. Like the Alberta, she went into service in the spring of 1884.

It didn't take Sir Alexander Galt, owner of the Galt coal mines at Lethbridge, and the instigator of the steamboat plan, long to discover his idea might not be as good as he'd thought.

"In 1884," he wrote gloomily "I waited at Medicine Hat for water till after the twenty-fourth of May, and by the twenty-eighth of June our boats and barges were tied up for the season."

The steamers had moved hundreds of tons of coal, but Galt realized the idea just wasn't going to work.

In 1885, Alberta's "navy" reappeared in the history books when they were pressed into service to help troops fighting the Riel rebellion.

Unfortunately, they proved no more satisfactory in this venture than in the coal business. Indeed, all three captains were written off by their military bosses as "incompetent".

In retrospect, that judgment was more than unfair. Even at the time, not all of the military men agreed with it.

By 1886, the Baroness and Alberta had both been beached and dismantled. The little Minnow survived until 1898, as a lumber tug, then she too was scrapped.

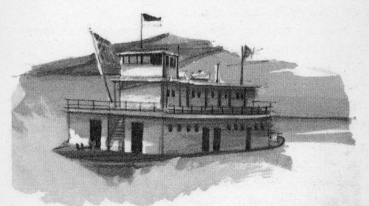

The remains of the Alberta clung to the shore of the river at Lethbridge for years.

For a while she was a playground for children, then

reduced to her ribs, a diving platform. Then she sank into the mud, and disappeared.

The idea of steamboats for Alberta was a bold one. And, in a period when so many bold ideas were paying off, it is rather sad that this one didn't.

* * * *

ONE HUGE MARSHALLING YARD . . .

The job of opening Alberta that started with the bull trains on the Whoop-Up Trail in the 1860's was finally completed by the arrival of the railroads in the 1880's and 1890's.

For a while, in the late 1870's, it seemed we might be in danger of having more railroads than people, and a province that was going to become one huge marshalling yard.

Fortunately for historians (and unfortunately for most of the Albertans who bought railroad stock), the early battle finally resolved itself with the Canadian Pacific winning out east-to-west, and the Grand Trunk — after some persistent fighting with Canadian Northern — winning out north-to-south.

It would be nice, here, to be able to tell the whole exciting story of railroading in Alberta. How Lady Macdonald, wife of Canada's prime minister, set off on a scenic tour of the Rockies with her chair perched on the cowcatcher of a speeding train. How Canadian Northern passengers would stand on the rear observation platform of the line's trains and watch, with a great deal of uneasiness, as the rails behind floated up and down like logs at sea.

And the proud story of how the citizens of Rimbey, when they decided they wanted a railroad, went out and built it — 35 miles of track and a train they called the "Peanut Special".

But it is simply too big a story. So, instead, we'll reach into the bag of railroad yarns and pull out just two small tales: of Edmonton's stuttering engineer and of a ghost train.

* * * *

D-D-DID I DO SOMETHING WRONG? . . .

Lin Bell was a big man — six foot three — and he was a railroad engineer. Indeed, if ever Alberta had an engineer who could be described as "the" engineer, Lin Bell might well be the man.

His story doesn't belong to the earliest days of railroading.

Lin started working for Canadian National out of Edmonton in 1916, and stayed with them until he retired in 1947.

And right from the first time Lin settled his 280 pounds behind the throttle of a CN locomotive, the company realized that the most anyone would ever be able to do to keep Lin Bell under control was to simply stay out of his way.

He could coax CN's startled old engines into feats of speed they'd never dreamed of — and broil a steak in the firebox while he was doing it.

Freight or passenger, he didn't care. As far as he was concerned, it was his heaven-ordained duty to get his trains where they were going in the shortest possible time.

On one early run with a passenger train, he had a conductor behind him who didn't like speed at all. Indeed, he got nervous if anyone even used the word.

So Lin pulled the train out of Edmonton and started to build up steam and speed. When Lin hit 72 miles an hour, the conductor's nerves finally gave out. The fright-ened man staggered forward through the coaches bobbing and weaving in the wake of Lin's engine, and finally made it to the front of the train.

Lin was waiting, and as soon as the infuriated conduc-tor appeared, he shook his head sadly and pointed out: "G-G-George, th-th-there's no use asking me to go any faster. I'm r-r-r-running as fast as the engine will go."

As Lin's reputation as a high-baller grew, CN began making meek but persistent appeals for him to slow down. Lin would promise faithfully to do just that — then go out and move his trains faster than ever.

Hauling a freight to Edson one night, Lin had his old engine wide open when a car jumped the track and de-railed 25 cars behind it. When everything finally stopped moving, the rest of the train crew came looking for Lin to point out the imminent possibility that his damn-fool speed was about to get them all fired.

They found Lin, wide-eyed, contemplating the wreck-age. "S-s-say," he mused philosophically, "it's a good th-th-thing we weren't going very fast."

Probably the favorite Lin Bell story is the one Tony Cashman tells of the engineer in his book The Edmon-ton Story.

Magistrate J. W. McCulla and an Edmonton lawyer were standing on the station platform at Stony Plain when "A sound as of distant artillery, a singing in the rails, and a trembling of the platform signalled the approach of Lin Bell pulling freight. The roar increased and the train plummetted past the station.

"Well, it got halfway past anyway. Then a switch opened and the last fourteen cars ran off on to a siding and turned into a pile of wooden sticks of miscellaneous sizes. Lin got his engine stopped well on toward Edmonton.

"As he walked back towards Stony Plain he called out: 'D-d-d-did I do anything wrong?' "

* * * *

THE GHOST OF 1908 . . .

Railroad men are a superstitious lot, and you can believe this story or not. But you won't be able to deny, as Ken Liddell pointed out when he recorded the story for The Calgary Herald, that "something strange happened" on the line between Medicine Hat and Dunmore in the summer of 1908.

"Bob Twohey was engineer and Gus Day the fireman on an engine travelling from Medicine Hat to Dunmore about eleven o'clock one night in June of that year," writes Mr. Liddell.

"At Dunmore they were to couple to the Spokane Flyer, which did not enter Medicine Hat, and take it west to Lethbridge and into the Crow's Nest Pass.

"They were two miles out of Medicine Hat when before them appeared a train approaching on the single line that wound around the cutbanks as it climbed a steep grade from the valley to the tableland of the prairie.

"As Gus Day recalled years later, the headlight of the approaching train seemed to be the size of a wagon wheel. The reflection ahead was as though the firebox was open on the locomotive of the approaching train.

"Day stood at the cab doorway and Twohey's hand remained suspended before the brake valve as a string of phantom coaches sped past. The coach windows were lighted and crew members waved a greeting from places where crew members would be expected to be found waving greetings as trains passed.

"And then the phantom disappeared. Twohey and Day each fearful of what the other may have thought had they expressed feeling, said nothing.

"Two weeks later, Twohey and Day met on a street in Medicine Hat. Feeling safer with the passage of time perhaps, they found courage to ask each other about what each had seen that startling night.

"Each was thankful to learn the other had witnessed the same sight and had experienced the same eerie feeling.

"But it worried Twohey. He told Day he had been to a 'reader', meaning a fortune teller, and had been told that he would die within the month.

" 'I'm going to lay off for a couple of trips,' said Twohey. Day stayed on the job. A few nights later Day was on the same engine, going about the same duties. This time the engineer was J. Nicholson replacing Twohey who had booked off.

"At exactly the same spot the phantom train again appeared, headed toward them with whistle blowing and headlight burning. And again it simply evaporated into the darkness as its crew members again waved greetings from their positions on its engine and cars.

"On the morning of July 8, Day reported for duty and found he was assigned to yard service. H. Thompson took his place as fireman on the engine that made a morning trip to Dunmore to pick up the Spokane Flyer, but this time to take it east to Swift Current. The engineer was J. Nicholson. They left Medicine Hat and headed into the hills.

"About 100 yards from the spot where the phantom train had been seen on two different nights and by two different crews, another train appeared around the curve, headed straight for them.

"This time it was daylight and it was for real. It was No. 514, the passenger train coming in from Lethbridge. And the man at the throttle was Bob Twohey, who had overcome his fears and had returned to work.

"The inevitable happened. The outbound engine and inbound passenger train collided. The wreck took the lives of Twohey and Nicholson, the engineers, both of whom had earlier seen the phantom train at almost the same spot. It also took the lives of a fireman named Gray and a conductor named Mallett, on the in-bound passenger train, and seven of the passengers.

"Thompson, fireman on the out-bound engine, escaped by jumping. He recalled later that just before the crash he had seen a farmer standing on a hill, waving his arms. The farmer could see both engine and passenger train, and realized a crash was inevitable. Thompson had mistaken the farmer's frantic armwaving to be the usual friendly greeting . . ."

* * * *

Alberta's aviation age is still unfolding. But already it is building a history of its own.

And that history is accumulating as many legends as the railroads that came before.

It has a young woman flyer named Katherine Stinson giving Alberta its first airmail flight, from Calgary to Edmonton, in 1918.

It has Captain Fred McCall pioneering commercial aviation in the province when he flew a load of nitroglycerine in to help blow out an oil fire at Turner Valley in 1927.

It has Wilfred "Wop" May, one of the hardy breed of bush pilots who opened northern Alberta with their little airplanes. May himself made aviation history with a 700-mile winter flight to carry vital drugs to a stricken Fort Vermilion, and had a crowd of 2,000 waiting to cheer him when he returned to Edmonton.

But there is one story, unknown to most people in Alberta, that marked the real beginning of aviation in the province and that established the spirit of our growing air age.

* * * *

ALBERTA'S FORGOTTEN FLYER . . .

Ask most people when aviation started in Alberta and they'll guess somewhere after the First World War. And they'll be wrong.

It started in 1906, in the basement of a care-free Edmonton bachelor named Reginald Hunt.

Hunt was handy with his hands, and a bit of an inventor. Like most people, he'd heard of airplanes and was excited about the idea of flight.

And it didn't seem at all impractical to him to go one step further and create an airplane of his own.

It took him three years, but he did just that.

The first step, he decided, was to design a glider. With the help of a carpenter friend, and months of labor, he gradually created a monster of pipe and big flat wings and a tail-assembly that looked like a huge box kite. It had four bicycle wheels under it; two big ones under the wings and two small ones under the strange-looking tail.

And one day he ran the whole improbable contraption off a ramp and it glided gently through the air for a few feet. The blasted thing actually flew.

Most people would have been satisfied with that, but not Hunt. He wanted a real honest-to-God powered airplane.

What he needed was a motor, so he built one. It took a whole winter of effort, but he designed and hand-crafted an airplane engine.

Then he set to work and designed and hand-crafted a propeller. It had four blades and, as Hunt explained later, "I based my design on the fans that keep flies from sleeping in restaurants."

Hunt was still working on his flying machine when, on Feb. 23, 1909, James McCurdy made Canada's first recorded flight over the ice at Baddeck Bay, Nova Scotia. McCurdy had managed to stay in the air for about two minutes.

Hunt didn't pay any attention to the feat. He was too busy.

Finally, at two o'clock on the afternoon of Labor Day in 1909, Hunt was ready. He rolled his invention to a field in west Edmonton, strapped himself in, and . . . well, we'll let Tony Cashman explain what happened next:

"The engine started all right . . . he stepped it up . . . it turned faster and faster still running smoothly . . . the propellers hummed evenly . . .

"Hunt shut his eyes and opened the throttle wide. The plane lurched forward, and after a short run across the open field it was in the air. Hunt had calculated well. The controls worked just as he figured they would. The control surfaces were large and it was much like sailing a boat, only Reginald Hunt was sailing in a realm where no boat had sailed before, not in Western Canada anyway."

Hunt managed to keep his airplane flying, 35 to 50 feet above the ground, for an incredible 35 minutes — totally eclipsing McCurdy's record set six months earlier.

This pioneer flyer spent years trying to interest backers in the idea of an aviation industry for Alberta. But people, even though he'd already proved otherwise, just said it "would never get off the ground."

So Reginald Hunt ended his days, a forgotten man, building boats in northern Alberta.

But what he did over Edmonton that afternoon in 1909 set the spirit of a transportation history that is still unfolding in Alberta . . .

* * * *

RESOURCE DEVELOPMENT

"The colonizers had brought with them their wood-burning cook stoves. Fuel was scarce. There were only a few cottonwood trees, willows and birch brush on the creek. Consequently, President Card, John A. Woolf and George L. Farrell set out to look for coal . . .

"A small vein of coal was found about three miles up the creek which was opened up on June 18th and which provided all with greater comfort." (Recollection of a Cardston pioneer)

BLACK NUGGETS . . .

It was 1870 and Alberta was still counting her natural resources in beaver pelts and buffalo hides.

Few of the traders gave much thought to the fact some of the more enterprising Montana ranchers were beginning to drift small herds onto the thick buffalo grass of the Alberta prairie. Fewer still knew that a settler named Francis Willock, at what would become Pincher Creek, had found a few grains of wheat in his pocket and — out of curiosity — planted them.

In the north, Hudson's Bay men simply shrugged off Cree stories of a sandy place where black tar seeped from the ground.

But, during that year of 1870, a young Irishman named Nicholas Sheran was plodding north on the trail from Fort Benton, in Montana, to the trading post of Fort Whoop-Up in southern Alberta.

Like so many other young men of the time, Sheran had the gleam of gold in his eye. He had visions of gravel bars in fast-flowing streams where a man could reach in and pull out shining nuggets, of swirling pans of sand that would yield rich flecks of yellow dust.

Like so many other young men of the time, Sheran would find his golden dream empty. But, unlike the others, he would stumble onto a dream to replace it, and start one of Alberta's major resource industries.

Even before he reached his destination of Fort Whoop-Up, Sheran had noticed black outcroppings along the shore of the Belly River. When he investigated, he discovered it was coal.

To a man interested in gold, however, coal isn't very exciting stuff. Sheran just filed the information away in his mind and pushed on north.

It took only a few months of prospecting to convince Sheran that southern Alberta wasn't gold country. But his prospecting trips hadn't been entirely a waste. All along the riverbanks near Fort Whoop-Up, Sheran kept on finding thick outcroppings of black coal.

Gradually, an idea took shape in his head. If a man could get a little backing, and was willing to work hard, it might be possible to mine that coal and ship it south to Fort Benton — which was becoming a main service and transport centre.

When Sheran approached some of the other prospectors about the idea, their comments were discouraging. Coal was nothing but hard work for little money. And anyway, no one could move enough wagonloads of coal along the rutted trail south to make it worthwhile.

Sheran was stubborn, but he was quickly running out of cash. So he built a crude shack near Fort Whoop-Up and began operating a ferry service across the Belly River.

Ferry traffic was light, and Sheran had enough time to continue probing the black outcroppings. Gradually he began building an operation to meet the heating needs of the fort and the growing number of settlers in the area.

For two years, Sheran struggled on. Then, in 1872, at a place later to be known as Sheran's Crossing, he discovered a new thick seam of coal in the side of a hill.

He began chipping away at the seam, following it into the hill. Almost unwittingly, Sheran was digging the first underground mine in Alberta.

The seam ran on and on. Soon Sheran's team of bulls were a common sight on the Whoop-Up Trail as they trudged south the 200 miles to Fort Benton with loads of coal.

Sheran coal sold at $3 a ton at the mine entrance, at $15 a ton in Fort Macleod, and at $22 a ton in Fort Benton.

Sheran, however, wasn't getting rich. He couldn't get the backing to make his mine — only half a mile from where Lethbridge's high-level bridge now stands — realize its potential.

All Sheran could do was struggle along, with hardly a cent in his pocket, and hope his luck would turn some day.

In 1882, it finally did, but it was a tragic turn for the worse.

Sheran was helping a party of North West Mounted Police to cross the flooding Belly River when his horse slipped and threw him into the water. He disappeared without a trace.

Sheran died a tragic figure. Even in death, he remained to his contemporaries "a stubborn Irish fool who didn't have the sense to give up."

Eighty-five years later, however, The Lethbridge Herald would remember Nicholas Sheran in another way:

"Sheran died a poor man, and like many others who have made great contributions to their country, failed to see the results or reap the rewards of his efforts.

"Little did he realize that he had pioneered an industry which was to form the backbone of Lethbridge."

* * * *

THE BIG DIG . . .

The real tragedy of Nicholas Sheran was that he died just a little too soon. By 1882, eastern capital was finally getting stirred up at the idea of a coal industry in the west.

The North Western Coal and Navigation Company had been formed, with Sir Alexander Galt — one of the fathers of Confederation — as its guiding force.

At his instigation, and that of his son, Elliot, the company sent two men named William Stafford and Capt. Nicholas Bryant west to look over the coal lands.

The two did extensive prospecting, and the reports they sent back excited the Galts. In a matter of months, the Galts were on the scene personally to check the finds.

Soon Sir Alexander was on his way to England to raise money, and Elliot was hard at work laying the foundations of the Galt mining empire that would give birth to Lethbridge.

William Stafford became the first superintendent of the operation, and it was he who persuaded the Galts to locate their mines on the east bank of the Belly River rather than the west shore that Sheran had been mining.

He knew that transportation of the coal was vital to the success of the enterprise, and that any mines operating across the river would face serious problems. There were no bridges and getting the coal to market would be an insurmountable problem.

At Stafford's advice, the miners went to work on the east side, sinking the first tunnel into the river bottom approximately where the high-level bridge now stands.

Originally, the Galts expected the settlers to be their main market, but the arrival of the trans-continental line of the CPR changed that.

The CPR tested the coal and found it excellent for use in their steam locomotives. North Western was given a substantial order — on the condition it would build a railway line to connect the mine with the CPR route.

This was done, and the narrow-gauge "turkey track", as it came to be called, was running tons of coal eastward by August, 1885.

The task of raising coal from the river bed was becoming increasingly difficult, despite construction of an inclined railway. The company turned to shaft mines. Galt No. 1 was followed in steady succession by Galt No. 2, then 3, 4, 5 and 6.

The hook-up with the CPR line, in addition to the direct business with the railway, opened all of Canada to the North Western complex.

In an effort to keep up with the demands, the Galts even tried the short-lived experiment of building three steamers to barge coal down to Medicine Hat. Impossible navigation conditions, however, soon put an end to the project.

The success of the Galt operation was drawing competitors by the score. Soon all Alberta was being probed for coal and mine after mine was opening. Almost overnight, there were strings of shafts all through the Crows Nest Pass, at Diamond City, and around the present city of Drumheller.

The western coal-mining business seemed to offer everyone a chance to make a fortune, so everyone came to make it.

But if the hastily-formed mining companies were developing one of Canada's major resources, they were also setting the scene for disaster.

* * * *

THE CRASH OF TURTLE MOUNTAIN . . .

The Galt coal-mining operation around Lethbridge was a carefully-engineered, safety-conscious operation.

Unfortunately, many of the other early operations were not. Reckless for profits, operators became reckless of lives, and they hurled miners into shafts that were poorly dug and poorly braced. Some of those shafts would have made better graves than tunnels. And some of them did . . .

The Indians always had a secret dread of Turtle Mountain in the Crows Nest Pass. They called it "the mountain that moves", and they would never camp at its base.

Unfortunately, Samuel Gebo and H. L. Frank didn't take Indian superstition seriously.

Coal had been discovered in Turtle Mountain in 1900 by a man named Henry Pelletier of Blairmore. Lacking capital, Pelletier had sold his claim to Gebo, a promoter with mining experience.

Gebo brought in Frank, a wealthy speculator from Butte, Montana, and by 1901, shifts of miners were burrowing into Turtle Mountain and a small town named Frank was taking shape at the foot of "the mountain that moves".

The objective of the mine was production of 1,000 tons a day, and the owners pushed their men recklessly to reach it. Sound engineering and safety rules were ignored.

By the spring of 1903, the miners had dug 5,000 feet into Turtle Mountain, ripping out seams of coal 9 to 12 feet wide in a long, upstretching tunnel.

It is easy, looking back, to gape in horror at the incredible stupidity building to a terrible climax in Frank. The men who climbed to the top of Turtle Mountain — and men did regularly — should have wondered at the long crack in the top edge of the mountain; a crack that was widening daily.

And the men working inside the mine itself should have wondered at the strange things happening there. There had been a minor quake the year the mine opened; there had been a series of small cave-ins. Two-foot timbers set one night would be found smashed to matchwood the next morning. Pockets of rock, emptied of coal, would be found mysteriously sealed a day or two later.

But, suddenly, it was 4 o'clock on the morning of April 29, 1903. Twenty miners were inside Turtle Mountain, a freight train was standing at the mine entrance, and more than 600 people lay sleeping in Frank. It was too late for wondering.

The engineer of the freight train, Ben Murgatroyd, and his two brakemen had just finished spotting a car and were preparing to leave the mine. They shouted farewells to the mine weighman and to two miners who had come out to the entrance to take a lunch break.

Then, abruptly, Murgatroyd heard a rock tear loose from high on the face of the mountain. He yelled a warning to the brakemen walking beside the engine and jammed the throttle wide open. The brakemen grabbed for the handrails and hung on desperately as the engine screamed down the grade from the mine and across a bridge.

Above them, they heard a terrifying roar as 70 million tons of rock — the whole face of Turtle Mountain — peeled loose.

In one minute and forty seconds it was all over. Everything was silent again.

Murgatroyd and his brakemen stood, staring in disbelief into the darkness. The bridge the engine had raced over, with sparks flying from its wheels, was gone.

The mine entrance was gone, and with it the three men who had been sitting there. Another 18 men were sealed inside the mountain itself.

In the valley below, most of the town of Frank, and the bodies of at least 66 men, women and children (the exact toll has never been determined), lay buried under a churning sea of rock.

In the hours and days that followed, the shadow of Turtle Mountain produced more heroes than any other town in Alberta history.

Men risked their lives to free those trapped in the

rocks that covered the town. Inside the mine, with the entrance and air shafts sealed, 18 gasping miners fought off deadly gas and dwindling oxygen to dig their way to freedom.

One of the brakemen, Sid Choquette, had run across the shifting rocks in utter darkness and successfully stopped the speeding Spokane Flyer, filled with passengers, before it could crash into the wall of rock across the main rail line.

But this isn't an account of heroism. It is an account of coal-mining and of an event that changed its shape forever.

Within a week of the disaster, investigators were pouring over the remains of Frank, demanding answers to questions of engineering and safety that no one could answer satisfactorily.

Samuel Gebo was ruined financially. H. L. Frank, haunted by the disaster, slowly went insane and died in a private sanatorium in 1908.

Unbelievably, the mine in Turtle Mountain was re-opened, but it was doomed. There were floods and fires, and Turtle Mountain continued to churn and heave.

Finally in 1910, after ownership of the mine had been sold to Canadian Coal Consolidated Limited, the Geological Survey of Canada warned that another slide could occur at any time. If it did, the government warned, the coal company would be held directly responsible.

Turtle Mountain, "the mountain that moves," was finally left in peace.

There have been other mining disasters, but the Frank Slide was the greatest single factor in creating the stringent safety regulations that forced so many opportunists to get out of the mining business.

And, inevitably, economic reality took over. The industry had seemed to offer everyone a chance to make a fortune, but the truth was that there is a limit to how much "fortune" there is in anything.

The remains of that shattered era are still there to see: at Frank, and in the tumbling mine buildings around Drumheller.

They can be seen, too, near Lethbridge in the grass-covered remains of Diamond City — of which The Lethbridge Herald said in 1911 that:

"There is probably no town or district in Alberta that has brighter prospects or greater resources . . ."

* * * *

THE STRUGGLE BACK . . .

The bad times that started with Turtle Mountain plagued Alberta's coal industry right up to the last decade.

In 1957, the last of the Galt mines closed. The Shaughnessy mines of Lethbridge Collieries followed in 1964. An effort to revive mining in Taber failed shortly afterward.

Markets for coal were shrinking as competition from oil and gas increased. The few coal companies still active were consolidating their holdings, closing down less profitable mines.

But, slowly, the coal industry has begun to climb back. Coal is, by a wide margin, the largest fuel reserve Canada has. As power and energy demands continue to grow, more and more industries are looking to coal to meet their needs.

Alberta power companies alone, for example, use more than 4 million tons of coal a year.

More important, possibly, than the increase in domestic demand, is the long-awaited breakthrough in export sales of coal.

For years, Alberta producers had fought to find a way to get to the enormous market in Japan. Finally, in 1969, the provincial government built a special spur of the Alberta Resources Railway to Grand Cache and in 1970 McIntyre Porcupine Mines Ltd. began shipments on a Japanese contract. The contract, to ship 30 million tons of coal over the next 15 years, is worth $450 million.

Which brings us back to Nick Sheran, chipping away at cutbanks on the Belly River with all the fury of his vision of a coal industry for Alberta.

It seems our coal industry has proved how right it was for him to be "a stubborn Irish fool who didn't have the sense to give up."

* * * *

Kootenai Brown was one of Alberta's most colorful explorers and characters; discovering among other things the scenic potential of the Waterton Lakes district.

But, for all that's known about him, few Albertans realize that he almost became our first oilman — all for the price of a horse.

Wandering the hills of southwestern Alberta in the 1890's, he and a friend called Lafayette French stumbled over a slough shiny with oil slicks.

Excited, they traded a horse for the rights to the spot and started drilling.

Unfortunately for Kootenai, the hole was dry. But the old explorer had started something: he'd started people thinking about oil.

* * * *

MEDICINE TO BURN . . .

A lot of people were talking about oil in the 1890's, but not too many were doing anything about it.

It took a stubborn old Waterton pioneer known as Uncle Bill Aldridge to really give the oil business its beginnings in Alberta.

The diary of one of the original Cardston settlers tells the story so well that it would be a shame to do anything more than pass it on the way we found it:

"Uncle Bill had heard of the oil seepage that was reputed to be somewhere in the vicinity of Waterton Lakes and he became determined to find it.

"One day in the summer of 1898 he and Oliver (his son) took their Winchesters, bedding, flour mixed with baking powder and salt, water pail and frying pan, and started from the cabin to find the oil. At noon they camped on Cameron Creek. Not far from the edge of the creek they kindled a fire and Oliver was sent to the creek for water.

"He was astonished when looking down at the edge, to see pools of what looked like black water, and called to his father come down and have a look at it.

"Bill came down, put his fingers into the black water, smelled it, tasted it and said, 'My gosh, boy, this is the ile we're lookin' for. Sure enough, it's ile.'

"He was then looking into what was later called Oil Creek, now Cameron Creek, and oil pools were lying in the wallows made by the bears when they came down to drink and rolled in the oil that seeped at the edge of the creek . . .

"Uncle Bill then laid a log across the creek to still the water and allow the oil to run out on top. To procure the oil, he laid gunny sacks on top of the water. The sacks absorbed the oil, which he then wrung out in buckets and barrels. Sometimes he boiled the oil to evaporate the water and to bring the oil to machine-oil consistency.

"This he carried in cans and barrels to Cardston, where he sold it to farmers to oil such conveyances and machinery as wagons, buggies, rakes, mowers and discs, and for other lubrication purposes. Sometimes he and his boys collected as much as 40 barrels a day from this seepage.

"For the Aldridge family, this crude oil had a medicinal value for such ailments as colds, pneumonia, sores, sunburn, blisters and 'the grip', by which name the flu was called in those days.

"At one time Uncle Bill became ill at the Hotel de Woolf. There was no doctor in town but nearly every family had a knowledge of the use of herbs and plasters with which to treat the sick.

"Mr. and Mrs. Woolf applied all their knowledge of herbs, plasters and nostrums to make him well, but nothing was of any avail.

"Finally, fearing he was going to die, Uncle Bill elected to be taken home where he could pass his last days with his family. The Woolfs, father and sons, made a comfortable bed of straw and blankets in the wagon bed, carried Uncle Bill there and snugly tucked him in, with a final warning to Oliver to drive slowly and carefully.

"When they reached the Belly River, 15 miles west of Cardston, Uncle Bill said, 'Boy, you'll have to stop. I can go no further.' Then he had an inspiration. 'Boy,' he said to Oliver, 'get me that bottle of ile out of the jockey box.'

"He tipped the quart bottle up and drank a half a pint of it. After an hour or two, with the oil acting as a purgative, he began to feel better. Oliver prepared supper over the campfire. His father ate hungrily and then said, 'Boy, hook up the horses and we'll go on home;' another 16 miles over rough roads.

"He then climbed to the spring seat beside Oliver and drove to his home where an anxious wife and children awaited him in alarm over his unusually long stay.

" 'That ile sure worked,' he said affectionately to Oliver in retelling the story to his family. 'It sure did,' said Oliver dryly."

It didn't take long for businessmen to hear of Bill Aldridge's oil find. Offers poured in, and finally, seven years after he found it, Uncle Bill sold off his Cameron Creek claim to the Vancouver Coal and Coke Company for $2,000 and 100,000 shares of stock.

The company drilled and struck oil at 1,100 feet. But they never were able to strike the main reservoir, and finally abandoned the project.

The rig burned down and the well eventually became a repository for garbage and junk.

But, at Cameron Creek, the oil still flows on the water. And, any time you want to, you can go down, stick your finger in the black water, smell it, taste it, and — in memory of Bill Aldridge — holler: "My gosh, boy, this is the ile we're lookin' for!"

* * * *

IT'S A GAS . . .

Oil may have been what Uncle Bill was after, but across the province other exciting discoveries were being made.

So exciting, in fact, that the mayor of Medicine Hat forgot to put his clothes on.

In 1892, a CPR crew drilling for water 30 miles west of Medicine Hat was astonished when its well caught fire.

They had discovered natural gas.

Industry attracted by the find would make Medicine

Hat the Pittsburgh of the west, predicted the townspeople.

Under Mayor W. T. Finlay, the town council authorized the drilling of more gas wells.

But when the first well in Medicine Hat reached 1000 feet below the ground, all the money was gone — and still not a whiff of gas.

Mayor Finlay gambled and ordered the drillers to keep going.

Ten feet deeper, gas under great pressure blew the drill out of the ground with a mighty roar.

The blow-out occurred early in the morning while the mayor was dressing. He didn't bother to finish.

Braces blowing in the wind, he ran toward the hissing well.

The informally-attired mayor was soon joined by a throng of citizens celebrating the discovery of a resource that would soon make the town and the province famous.

* * * *

OLD GLORY AND OTHERS . . .

By 1908, the Calgary Natural Gas Company, under Archibald Dingman, had drilled a successful gas well on the Colonel James Walker estate in east Calgary.

Enough gas was produced to service some homes, provide a few street lights, and supply the Calgary brewery.

But this didn't satisfy Eugene Coste who acquired Dingman's company and, in 1911, founded the Canadian Western Natural Gas, Light, Heat and Power Company.

Coste was determined his company would live up to its name.

Old Glory, a well on the Bow Island gas field, had blown in for Coste in 1909, earning him the title of "father of the natural gas industry".

Coste then undertook the mammoth task of constructing a 16 inch gas transmission pipeline from Bow Island to Calgary — a distance of 170 miles.

The pipeline — the third longest in North America, and the longest of its diameter — was completed in 86 days; good time even by today's standards.

Lethbridge, Calgary, Fort MacLeod, Granum, Claresholm, Nanton and Okotoks were connected with the main line, which became the backbone of the natural gas company's present operations in southern Alberta.

But the best was yet to come.

* * * *

SLICK BUSINESS . . .

For Albertans in 1914, the rainbow's end was Turner Valley.

Oil may not have the same aesthetic value as gold, but its value in dollars and cents was enough to turn Calgary into a city of lunatics.

"It was the wildest, most delirious, most uproarious, most exciting time that had ever entered into human imagination to conceive," exclaimed the Calgary Albertan.

Overnight, everyone became a "shareholder" — some filing claims in such unlikely spots as Bowness Park, now in Calgary.

And, just as fast, most of them went broke.

Five hundred "oil companies" sprang up instantaneously. Of the 50 companies that even made an attempt at drilling for oil, few were even mildly successful.

Within a few months, most of the big oil promoters had slunk away, their pockets bulging.

Calgarians had parted with more than a million dollars of their savings.

What they had to show for it were thousands of worthless share certificates — which some enterprising souls eventually used to wallpaper their homes and even a hotel lobby.

It wasn't that there was no oil at Turner Valley — but the excitement and speculation accompanying the 1914 discovery were out of all proportion to the actual find.

Even though Turner Valley was Canada's first commercial oil discovery in 50 years — and the first ever in the west — the field was producing a meagre average of less than 20 barrels of oil a day.

The man behind the hysteria over this comparative trickle of oil was a persistent optimist called William Stewart Herron.

Herron came from Ontario to settle on a farm in Okotoks in 1903.

Dreams of wealth nagged at the dissatisfied farmer. When the gas seep bubbling through Sheep Creek which flowed across his land turned out to be not marsh gas but petroleum, Herron was ecstatic.

After some shrewd property dealings, he had the money to secure oil leases in Turner Valley.

"I knew — or at least I thought I knew, which amounts to the same thing — that there was oil in the Valley," Herron was said to have remarked.

* * * *

PETROLEUM COMES OF AGE . . .

It was almost inevitable that Herron would get together with a man of equal ambition, Archibald Dingman.

In 1912, the pair formed Calgary Petroleum Products Company and agreed to spend $50,000 to drill a well.

Their decision couldn't have been more timely.

South of the border Henry Ford had begun to make automobiles in a big way. Throughout North America the need for new oil sources was far outstripping the supply.

The sun had risen on the petroleum industry.

But drilling for oil, Dingman and Herron discovered, was a tedious procedure.

Their "Discovery" well — the one that caused the furore of 1914 — was a teaser. It yielded a respectable amount of oil, but refused to come up with the "gusher" everyone was waiting for.

Dramatic reports of their progress, however, carried by Calgary newspapers, maintained a fever pitch of interest among the citizens.

Only a few saw through the frantic "get-rich-quick" schemes which had become the local obsession.

"The trouble with this oil situation at this formulative stage," Bob Edwards wryly suggested in his Calgary Eye Opener, "is that you are never sure whether the man you meet on the street is a multi-millionaire, or just an ordinary, common millionaire."

When Dingman and Herron's "Discovery" well made its modest debut May 14, 1914, the ordinary common millionaires were left out in the cold.

As the overnight oil companies faded away with fat wallets, and sadder but smarter Calgarians turned their attention to the coming of war, Dingman and Herron continued their search for the big gusher.

The Turner Valley story had just begun.

* * * *

OIL TO BURN . . .

It was ten years before another major discovery was made in the valley, but between 1924 and 1936, 114 wells were drilled in the area.

Most of the natural gas was being burned off in enormous flares consuming 600 million cubic feet per day. The wastage was equal to nearly one third of Canada's natural gas consumption in 1969.

But what the early Turner Valley oilmen did not know was they were only skimming the surface.

Below the cap of gas they were burning off in vast amounts lay a pool of more than a billion barrels of crude oil.

Risking their combined life savings, three Calgarians, R.A. Brown, George Bell and J.W. Moyer, drilled the well which revealed this pool in 1936.

But the damage had been done.

Years of burning off the gas flares had dwindled away the gas pressure needed to bring the oil to the surface.

Petroleum engineers estimate that, instead of half a billion barrels, only 120 million will eventually be extracted from the Turner Valley pool.

It was a costly lesson for Alberta, but the mistake has not been repeated.

What of the two men who were in on the beginning of it all?

William Herron finally became a millionaire in 1926 when the Turner Valley leases he had clung to so tenaciously made good.

But the stock market crash of 1929 and the ensuing depression robbed him of his fortune, and he died in poverty 10 years later.

Devoted to his motto "Carry on; we want and need more

oil", Archibald Dingman continued to make his living from small Turner Valley oil finds.

But Dingman died three months before the discovery of the huge Turner Valley oil pool in 1936, too soon to see the truth in his oft-spoken words.

* * * *

THE SEARCH GOES ON . . .

By the end of World War II, dreams of gigantic oil fields in Alberta were dwindling fast — as were the finances to support oil explorations.

After years of drilling with nothing to show but 133 dry holes, Imperial Oil decided to invest in one last try.

The company chose a location west of the Viking gas field, which supplies Edmonton with natural gas.

Imperial Leduc No. 1 got off to a discouraging start on the farm of Mike Turta.

But as the drillers reached the 5,000 foot level their hopes began to rise.

On February 3, 1947 oil squirted out of the well to a height of 70 feet, drenching the triumphant crew.

Imperial realized it had discovered the first oil in western Canada in 11 years.

Two months later, the company had an even bigger find on its hands, Leduc No. 2.

Just a mile and a half southwest of Number 1, the second well yielded the best pay section yet found in Canada.

* * * *

THE RICHEST SANDBOX IN THE WORLD . . .

Sidney Clark Ells set off on a 250 mile hike from Edmonton to Fort McMurray in 1913 and returned with samples of what would soon become the world's most valuable sandbox.

The Athabasca Tar Sands contain enough potential oil to meet Canada's needs for oil (based on 1969 requirements) for 700 years.

Suspecting the vast promise of the bituminous sands, Ells shipped out 60 tons of the tar sands from McMurray to Edmonton in the winter of 1915.

The sand was moved by horse team "in temperatures ranging from 20 to 50 below zero without tents for men or horses."

Ells' cargo was used to pave Edmonton streets — pavement which was still being used 50 years later.

But the dilemma posed by the tar sands was how to separate the oil from the sand.

In the decades that followed Ells' expedition, many schemes were tried without success.

It was not until 1962 that Great Canadian Oil Sands Ltd. won a government permit to start production from the sands.

They had the technical know-how. All they needed was the money.

With backing from Sun Oil, the company launched a project which would eventually cost them $250 million and produce 45,000 barrels of oil per day.

Five hundred government, oil industry and press representatives flew to the dedication of the GCOS plant at Fort McMurray in September 1967.

Already the plant was processing synthetic crude oil which would soon begin its journey along the 3,000 mile pipelines to refineries in Ontario and Ohio.

Seated at the head table among the dignitaries was Sidney Ells who made the first, most difficult journey to the Athabasca Tar Sands 54 years ago.

* * * *

With the promise of ample petroleum in the foreseeable future added to Alberta's other vital resources, economic progress in the province is assured for years to come.

Half of Canada's mineable coal exists in Alberta as well as abundant hydro-electric power.

The petroleum industry, through the development of an important fertilizer operation, has spurred the growth of agriculture.

Together, these two furnish the necessary ingredients for another boon to the economy: manufacturing.

The ups and downs of the oil industry have taken their toll on many Albertans.

Men lost their life savings.

Some, like William Herron, gained and lost several fortunes during the years of wild speculation.

Big oil companies invested millions of dollars in barren ground.

But, appropriately enough, the town of Leduc has coined the phrase which sums up the real story of oil in Alberta: "Oil's well that ends well."

* * * *

"In Lethbridge the housewife has the advantage of electricity at a low rate, and she may use it from early in the morning until midnight. She cooks, irons, sews, and can do a hundred things a day with its aid and it greatly lessens household duties" (The Lethbridge Herald, 1911)

* * * *

THE HARD DARK DAYS . . .

Alberta pioneers endured many hardships in settling the new land of the west; hardships that were compounded by isolation.

Well into the present century, settlers here were still far behind eastern Canada in many of the amenities we now all take for granted — mail, telephone and telegraph service, fashion, entertainment.

And if the settlers were being left in the dark in a cultural sense, they were being left "in the dark" in a literal sense as well.

In 1911, Albertans had electrical service in only the most rudimentary sense, and most didn't have it at all. A few cities, like Calgary, were using steam generators to bring a dim glow to life. In a few towns, enterprising individuals were using primitive equipment to offer a handful of customers sporadic "Saturday night and Monday morning" service.

But in most communities — and in all of rural Alberta — there was no electricity at all. These were the hard dark days. And for the farm family, because of sparseness of population and high development costs, the days would remain hard and dark for at least two decades longer.

Ten years ago, a writer named Mary Ellen Bradley painted a picture of a "typical" farm family of the era before power, and showed vividly how great a difference electricity makes to the quality of life:

"Mr. Farmer," she wrote, "started his day at dawn by hand-milking the five cows, feeding the pigs and horses. He separated the milk, using a hand-turned separator. Water for all the livestock had to be pumped by hand; though later a gas engine was purchased for the pump, but it proved unreliable and balky to start — especially on winter mornings.

"Meanwhile, the lady of the house had started her day, too. She was busy emptying ashes from the messy wood stove, carrying wood, building a fire to cook the meal and heat the house. Periodically the stove would refuse to burn the fuel properly, and smoke would fill the house.

"This was official notice that it was time to clean out the stove pipe, a major operation in any household. All the pipes would be taken down — gingerly handled, so as not to drop soot in the house — carefully carried out and away from the house, and then pounded to knock out the soot. In spite of the careful handling, when the job was done there usually would be a coating of dirty black soot over everything.

"Mrs. Farmer, among her many duties, assumed the responsibility of looking after the chickens; often as many as

200. Since a commercial hatchery was unheard of in those days, a small incubator, made of redwood, was kept warm by a coal-oil lamp.

"The eggs had to be turned every day, the lamp refueled, drafts screened off the eggs — and away from the lamp as well; of course, there was the constant danger of the lamp being blown out and the eggs ruined.

"When the small chicks were put in the brooder house a careful watch had to be kept on the heater — also non-electric — to see that it didn't become either too hot and smother the chicks, or too cold and allow them to freeze.

"When they first moved to the farm, Mrs. Farmer churned all the butter for the family with a dash churn. A few years later, the couple were able to buy a really modern convenience — a churn with a crank. So that she would not have to churn every day, she made a crockful of butter at a time, and put it into the well to keep it cool.

"Mr. Farmer had dug this well close to the house, about 25 feet deep, and 4 feet square. Food was put in pails or jars, a rope tied to the pail-handle or pail, or around the jar, and the whole thing was lowered into the natural 're-frigeration' of the well. It was only possible to keep fresh meat for a few days — butter and cream would keep for a few weeks.

"Keeping food, especially in summer was extremely difficult . . . Without home freezers, the Mason jar and canning kettles were part of the rituals of harvest.

"Mr. Farmer butchered the family's meat. Since a whole beef was too large for the family to use, half of the carcass was sold to a neighbor. (In some areas of the province, farmers joined in groups to form a 'ring', and butchered each others animals in turn for the group.)

"After the meat was butchered, Mrs. Farmer took over.

She cut the meat to fit into a quart jar, added salt, and secured the lid very tightly with a rubber jar ring. The jars were then put into a boiler or canning kettle and boiled for three hours.

"Preserving pork was quite a different process. First the meat was cured for three weeks in a brine made of saltpetre, salt, pepper and sugar. Then the pork was put into a wooden box to be smoked. A trench 8 to 10 feet was dug, a stove pipe laid along it and reaching into the box, a fire was built at the end of the trench about ten feet from the box. The smoke would draw through the pipe into the box where the meat was, giving it a nice smoky flavor."

Miss Bradley noted the difficulty of transportation, even for such routine matters as the weekly trip to the grocery store in town, then continued:

"Usually, after such a trip, they would arrive home much after dark and have to light the coal-oil lamps or lanterns. After all the rush and excitement to get away early that morning, it is quite possible the lamps had been forgotten, and would be out of oil. Then there would be fumbling in the dark until the oil can could be found, and further fumbling and spilling while filling the lamp.

"In the winter the lamps had to be filled every other day, or every day, depending on how early the family got up in the morning, and how long the lamps had to burn in the morning.

"Later, about 1928, a great improvement was introduced — the family acquired gasoline mantle lamps and a lantern utilizing the same principle. These gave off much better light than coal-oil lamps, but these also presented the same filling problem, complicated by the greater danger from the more explosive gasoline.

"And then, too, there was the exasperating problem of

delicate mantles which disintegrated when accidentally touched by clumsy fingers.

"One of Mrs. Farmer's most difficult chores was doing the family laundry. Her first washing aids were a wooden tub, a washboard and a hand-turned wringer. Then, several variations of hand-operated washing machines came on the market. Later, a washing machine with a gasoline engine was used. The water had to be hand-pumped and heated in a boiler on the stove.

"A sad iron — and they were properly named — was kept hot on the kitchen stove to iron all the clothes."

Given Miss Bradley's account, it is easy to understand why Alberta farm families chafed with impatience for the coming of electricity. And the account also provides a clue as to why so many farmers, even in the poverty years after the First World War, invested in the "extravagance" of a gasoline-powered generator.

* * * *

A FLICKER OF LIGHT . . .

If the farm family was suffering from lack of power in 1911, his neighbor in town wasn't doing much better.

In most small communities in Alberta, it was the era of the single light bulb and of part-time electricity.

One man, or a group of men, would invest in a generator — powered by gasoline or natural gas or, sometimes, a steam boiler — and go into the electrical business. As mentioned earlier, it was the day of "Saturday night and Monday morning" service.

Power was supplied only twice a week; on Saturday night for shopping in the stores, and on Monday morning for the housewives to use new electric washing machines to do the family laundry.

Even that part-time service, thanks to the unreliability of generating equipment, wasn't consistent. As unhappy customers soon discovered, it could often be as dark on Saturday night and Monday morning as it was the rest of the week.

And, for this sporadic service, customers were paying 25 or 30 cents a kilowatt hour — 10 to 15 times as much as electricity costs today.

* * * *

AND THEN A GLEAM . . .

But, in 1911, in Calgary, something was starting that would change the electrical scene in Alberta for good.

Calgary, like many other cities, was trying to meet its own power demands. It had first got electricity in the late 1880's, and the city had been struggling ever since to meet the expanding power requirements of industry and an exploding population.

Population growth alone — from 4,091 in 1901 to 43,-704 in 1911 — demonstrates vividly why the city, despite unceasing expansion of generating facilities, just couldn't keep up with the hunger for electricity.

By 1911, after three or four years of debate, the city fathers were wavering between an all-out expansion of their facilities, and the alternative of turning the whole mess over to some private company.

As it happened — far from accidentally — there was a "private company" waiting in the wings, eager to take over the job from the city.

As early as 1906, the Calgary Power and Transmission Company — which had among its backers R. B. Bennett (later Viscount Bennett) and W. Max Aitken (later Lord Beaverbrook) — had been working on a proposal that involved constructing a dam on the Bow River for hydro-electric power to supply Calgary.

By 1909, this company in combination with others, had proceeded to the stage of acquiring the rights to 1,000 acres of land at Horseshoe Falls from the Stony Indian Reserve. It had also arranged for the lease of water rights from the federal department of the interior, arranged an industrial contract in Exshaw — and a contract to supply power to Calgary.

That year, in order to simplify what was becoming a corporate nightmare, the backers created a new company — Calgary Power Company Limited — to handle the electrical business. The new company was officially registered in March, 1911.

Soon all the necessary agreements were signed and Calgary Power was in the position — not as enviable as it might have seemed — of trying to meet Calgary's electrical demands.

The key to the scheme was construction of the hydro plant at Horseshoe Falls. Work on the project had started in 1909, even before Calgary Power had been incorporated.

The deadline for completion was April 1, 1911 — a critical date if Calgary Power was going to be able to live up to its agreement with the city. As it turned out, the contract-or almost made it. He was a "mere" one month and twenty-one days late.

Calgary Power wasn't enchanted with the contractor, and the city fathers weren't enchanted with Calgary Power (nor would they be for many years), but the first hydro plant on the Bow was in operation, and the two tenuous wires linking Calgary to Horseshoe Falls would soon be woven into a web for a whole province.

* * * *

THE COWBOY LINEMAN . . .

"I guess," grins Henry Bradley, "that you could say that I was sort of a cowboy."

Which, in a strange kind of way, is precisely true.

Henry Bradley, today safety supervisor for Calgary Power, is a veteran of a unique period in the history of electrical power in Alberta. He is part of an era when a handful of men made it their personal responsibility to see that — no matter how impossible the odds — the people of Alberta got consistent and reliable electrical service.

The confidence with which you flip on your kitchen light is the lasting evidence of how well they succeeded.

Henry was a lineman and, as he says, "sort of a cowboy."

"The reason for this," he explains, "is that, at that particular time, you patrolled lines on horseback. I did it out of Calgary.

"You hired on to be sort of a tough guy, see; the idea being that if you couldn't repair it any other way you could bend it or make it work somehow or other.

"Patrolling the line, you'd usually be out maybe a week. You'd get your climbing irons — we called them galloping irons — and safety belt and gloves and stuff, tie them on back of the saddle and off you'd go.

"You'd eat and sleep at farm houses along the way.

"Horses were used to ride the lines right into the 40's. It was an excellent method of patrolling, because your attention was not necessarily distracted by having to drive or anything. The horse just took you along and away you went — as long as you were sufficient cowboy to stay there.

"The chap I hired from here was kind of a bronc buster himself, and what he used to do was rent three horses to the company. There was always two available, and one he was breaking.

"And when he got them half-broke, he gave them to the patrolmen to ride, to finish off the job. Then he could sell them off as saddle horses broke to ride.

"I can remember one time on one of those horses when I made it just as far as 4th St. and 8th Ave., where Eaton's is now, and the horse started to buck.

"This may be all right during Stampede time, but any other time you sure attract a lot of attention. I'll tell you, I sure scattered a lot of people when that horse decided to stand up on his two hind feet!

"People were yellin' 'Ride him cowboy!' and I thought, Oh Lord, if you only knew how little cowboy I really am! Made the job interesting, all right.

"I remember the first time I had to cross the Bow River down here on patrol. I wasn't just sure where they crossed the river on horseback, and I asked one of the CPR maintenance men who was stationed down there if he knew where the power patrolmen crossed the river.

" 'Right across there,' he says. So I looked at the river and I thought, well, he should know, and in I went.

"It was a good job I had a horse that was a strong swimmer. I got across with him goin' hard as he could and me hangin' on to his tail.

"It was a cold day, and I remember winding up at my destination where I was staying for the night just about literally frozen to the seat.

"When I caught up with that guy later, all he did was laugh and say I should have had more sense. True, I guess. Sometimes you've got to learn the hard way; get your knocks."

Henry pondered for a moment. "Strange thing, you know. I don't know whether we were really more self-sufficient then or what, but you didn't much think about the risks, the chance-taking.

"It was a risk being out on horseback in some of the weather we had to face, and we did some mighty chance-taking, working on those lines alone.

"But you never much thought about it. And if you did it just seemed an additional challenge.

"It was a duty you had to perform. Power must go on. It had to be restored. This was the thing, no matter how you had to do it.

"And when you'd get it repaired, you'd be relieved, and you'd think, well, you'd given a service. And that's what it was all about."

* * * *

THE FLICKERING YEARS . . .

For many long and difficult years after its birth in 1911, Calgary Power had to fight to survive. The reserves of water above the Horseshoe were far from stable. There was too much water in summer, and too little in winter. Even with the use of Calgary's Victoria Park steam generating plant, Calgary Power couldn't cope.

In winter, at Horseshoe, great slabs of ice would be sucked down and pinned against the intake, and the station would suddenly lose its generating load. Every available man on the staff would rush out with axes and poles and try to clear the obstruction.

Some of those men, in those trying days, found themselves with bundles of dynamite in hand and well on their way to becoming self-educated demolition experts.

The dynamite was for the ice, of course. But there were times, when Calgary's aldermen were complaining particularly loudly about flickering lights, that it was a sore temptation . . .

* * * *

GAHERTY TO THE RESCUE . . .

It was 1920, and Geoffrey Abbott Gaherty, chief engineer of Montreal Engineering Company Ltd., was on his way back to Montreal.

The owner of Montreal Engineering, I. W. Killam, had a small financial interest in an electric company called Calgary Power, and he asked Gaherty to take a look at the operation on his way back east.

Gaherty was the perfect man to "take a look at" a power company. Unlike most other engineers in Canada at that time, he had experience in the field. He'd been instrumental in Killam developments on Quebec's Gatineau River, and had done investigation work on the Nova Scotia Light and Power Company project.

Gaherty, as requested, stopped in Calgary to investigate the situation at Calgary Power. What he saw was hardly encouraging.

"At that time," as someone wrote later, "the company was in difficulty, power plants with no effective storage, producing unreliable power for only three customers, earning barely enough revenue to cover expenses, and its owners discouraged."

Gaherty, however, was interested in "potential", and he saw Calgary Power as a company with potential to spare.

Back in Montreal, he had a long discussion with Killam,

and Killam set to work to buy control of the ailing company.

As soon as he had it, he sent his chief engineer back to Alberta to bring Calgary Power to life.

It was Gaherty's engineering talent that inspired the projects that finally gave the company the generating reserves and stability it needed.

And, though few of those closest to him realized it at the time, Calgary Power was going to need amazing reserves and stability if it was going to live up to a dream Gaherty was nurturing.

Years later, a man who worked with Gaherty said that "he was a man who commanded admiration and respect from all who knew him."

It must have taken a great deal of both admiration and respect for those around Gaherty to accept the unbelievable targets he began setting in the early 1920's — a vastly-expanded generating network, an all-out bid to bring the majority of Alberta towns into a power system served by Calgary Power and, more astonishing still, an all-out bid to electrify rural Alberta.

It says something about the special quality of G.A. Gaherty to note that he wasn't immediately written off as insane. For "insane" is about the best word to describe the enormity — both financially and technically — of the projects Gaherty was proposing.

But those around Gaherty just said "Let's go," and the biggest gamble in Alberta history to that point (and possibly since that point) was underway.

Actually, Gaherty's plans were not as wild as they sounded. Technical improvements had now made long-range power transmission possible. Alberta's towns were beginning to grow, and with them their market potential — particularly since most towns were still suffering along with the

"Saturday night and Monday morning" quality of service.

If Calgary Power didn't reach out and make a try for the business, other companies might.

So, into the mountains of Banff late in the fall of 1922 went a party, led by Calgary Power surveyor J.E. Spurling, to investigate the potential of a power project to tap the Spray Lakes water resources. (Decades later that survey would finally find fruition in the Spray-Rundle-Three Sisters development.)

And spreading out across the province went other teams of men to look for routes for transmission lines.

In 1925, Managing Director Gaherty took to the road himself to woo Alberta's towns, to negotiate contracts and franchises, to purchase existing power-producing equipment (however terrible!), to negotiate easements through farms and ranches.

And at night he'd drive his Model T back over the rutted roads to Calgary and spend hours with his engineers; drawing plans for the dream that was rapidly taking shape.

In 1926 — with the hard-working, hard-fighting construction crews of McGregor Telephone and Power Construction Company still throwing up poles and line across the province — the first towns of High River, Olds and Blackie agreed to Calgary Power service.

That trickle of three became a stream of 15 more the next year, and a flood of 46 in 1928.

And, by then, the third part of the Gaherty dream — rural electrification — was already taking shape.

Earlier in this account of the development of electric power in Alberta, we turned to Mary Ellen Bradley's account of the hardships faced by Alberta farm families before electricity. We'd like to turn to her again to see the effects of what Gaherty was bringing.

"Talk of organizing rural electrification areas began to circulate. Canvassers covered the district to see how many farmers were in favor of obtaining central station power.

"When asked for an opinion, Mr. Alberta Farmer said with sudden conviction, 'I've waited forty years for power!'

"Mr. Farmer and his neighbors found a new use for co-operative 'bees' — they grouped together to clear brush for power line right-of-way. They had their homes wired. They began to haunt appliance dealers' showrooms and scan mail-order catalogs for the electrical appliances they would buy.

"With initial organization complete, crews from Farm Electric Services Ltd. appeared in the district. Miles of poles and wires began to spring up. Then, at last, the awaited day arrived — their transformer was connected and now they had ELECTRICITY!"

The key to the success of Gaherty's plans was "dependability". The economy of the new service was obvious to customers, but they had to be convinced that, unlike the power they'd had before, this new service was always going to be there when it was needed. If the power went off, and with it the heaters in a chicken hatchery . . .

"No one," a Calgary Power veteran recalled recently with a shudder, "knows just how thin we were stretched in those early days.

"If, even just once, our luck had gone bad . . ."

But it didn't go bad. And today only three cities — Edmonton, Lethbridge and Medicine Hat— handle their own generating requirements. A handful of other communities, including Calgary, own distribution systems.

Calgary Power's operation has expanded to 12 hydro plants (a 13th is now under construction) and 2 thermal plants on Lake Wabamun.

Between Calgary Power and its northern neighbor, Canadian Utilities, 99 per cent of all the farms in Alberta have electricity. There are 74,000 miles of transmission and distribution line in the province.

In 1964, when G.A. Gaherty died, J. E. Oberholtzer of Alberta's department of industry and development engraved his name in Alberta history with a few simple words:

"There is no need for special memorials for some people. In the case of Dr. Gaherty the power projects throughout the province of Alberta stand as permanent records of his achievements."

* * * *

COMMUNICATION

Struggling into the Rocky Mountains in July, 1841, Governor Sir George Simpson of the Hudson's Bay Company brought his party to an abrupt halt and began examining tree trunks.

It wasn't a search for firewood or a peculiar outbreak of "bush-fever". It was a desperate hunt for a letter.

Within minutes, Sir George's party had found what they were looking for. Scrawled in charcoal on the bark of a thick pine was a "picture-letter" telling them their guide, Edward Berland, and 27 sorely-needed horses were waiting at a nearby lake.

Yelling, cursing, and swatting at clouds of mosquitoes, the party hurried on. What they left behind, for nature to erase, may well have been the first "letter" in Alberta.

It would be ten years — 1851 — before Canada would have its first postage stamp (the famous three penny beaver). And it would be many more long years before the pioneers of Alberta knew what it was like to have the benefits of mail service.

* * * *

Actually, for 20 years after that party of Sir George's passed through on its mad dash to the Pacific, it didn't much matter that there wasn't any mail in Alberta.

Like Sir George, the only white men who had seen Alberta in the early years of the 1800's were mostly just passing through — usually in search of a badly-needed pass that would let the Hudson's Bay Company or the rival Nor'westers carry trade to the Pacific.

But here and there the rival trading companies were putting up posts to trade with the Indians. And with those posts came our first "settlers."

For these men of the trading posts, life was lonely in the extreme. They knew there was a world outside, but they didn't know much about what was happening in it.

True, now and then there would be a packet of mail tucked into a shipment of trade goods. But usually that mail would be only business instructions from headquarters — or notice that a party of explorers (of which there seemed a never-ending stream in those days) was on its way west.

And Jasper Hawes of Jasper House would up his prices a few beaver-skins, or sigh and clear a space on the floor for the trail-weary party soon to appear over the eastern horizon.

* * * *

THE RUMORED WEST . . .

If early westerners were getting little news about the east, easterners were getting all too much about the west. And most of it was, well . . . slightly distorted.

Enthusiastic accounts from explorers brought ill-equipped adventurers hurrying west in search of gold that often wasn't there. And those accounts sometimes plunged them into mountain "passes" that all too often literally ended in a stone wall.

* * * *

THE TRAGIC TRUTH . . .

Even while Palliser was probing the passes of the Rockies, gold was being found in the Fraser River. And news of the discovery brought easterners rushing west by the thousands.

The wiser made their way by boat, around the tip of South America and up the west coast. Others chose to go by land, confidently believing in reports that the way west was "an easy wagon road through a lovely country un-equalled for its beauty and salubrity of climate," and that the Rockies could be crossed "with perfect safety."

In the spring of 1862, a party of more than 100 Over-landers left Ontario for the golden west. They travelled by train to St. Paul and then to Fort Garry.

There, equipped with carts and provisions for 60 days, they set out across the prairies. With them was a pregnant woman and her two children; the youngest only three.

None of the party, of course, had given any thought to settling in Alberta — and what they encountered when they reached it did nothing to change their minds.

The prairies they found were a virtual swamp. It was raining when the Overlanders hit the plains, and it was still raining when they left them behind.

Many of the streams and rivers had spilled over their banks and were unfordable. The party had to work waist-deep in water to build temporary bridges that barely held together long enough to rush wagons across.

Hour after hour, they waded across the flooded meadows of Alberta. There were frequent sarcastic queries about when they would find the "overland" route they'd heard about.

For the eleven days it took to reach Fort Edmonton, they were never dry. They staggered in to the post "toil-worn, jaded, forlorn and tattered."

Fort Edmonton, however, was a sight that brought loud cheering from the party. Not only did it mean shelter. It meant to the misinformed 100 that they were almost at their destination. As one recalled later, "We had full confidence in our ability to reach the El Dorado of our hopes."

Months later, the ragged, starving survivors of that party straggled into the Cariboo. Behind them, they had left the memories of slaughtered animals and lost possessions. Behind them, too, they had left those who had lost the strength or will to go on.

And behind them, in the Rockies, they left graves. How many graves is something that they, and history, never recorded.

For those whose strength had carried them to the Fraser, there was no reward. Fate sent all away empty-handed.

All, that is, but the woman who made it to the Cariboo in time to give birth to a baby girl; the same brave woman who set out from Fort Garry so many months before on the "easy wagon road" to a western dream.

* * * *

THE "WHISKEY" EXPRESS . . .

In 1860, eastern Canadians were enjoying the amenities of parcel-post, registered letters and postal money orders, and — in Toronto at least — street letter boxes.

Albertans weren't jealous, for the simple reason that, since they still didn't have any kind of postal service themselves, they just didn't know what was happening in the east.

But in 1860, for southern Albertans at least, the times were about to start changing. A wild and wicked crew of men was on its way to the southern plains to do some trading. And, with the compliments of the U.S.A. — and a native thirst for whiskey — southern Alberta was about to get mail delivery.

Officially, the Hudson's Bay Company would NEVER trade liquor to the Indians. (Unofficially, of course, everyone had a good idea where all that rum in Alberta was coming from.) The free-traders of the northwest United States weren't that coy. They were out to trade whiskey for fur — and they didn't care who knew it.

When these free-traders found the U.S. government didn't approve of their practice, they simply headed north and began plying their trade with the Blackfoot in Canada.

So enthusiastic were the Blackfoot and Peigans that the traders soon had a steady stream of bullcarts squeaking back and forth between forts like Whoop Up in southern Alberta and Fort Benton in Montana. Heading south, the big carts were stacked high with buffalo robes and furs. Heading north, the principal cargo was whiskey — but, to the benefit of Alberta pioneers, tucked in among the barrels were precious pouches of mail.

The bull-carts had opened a channel of communication with the south and east. Albertans, for the first time, could begin to send and receive mail with some semblance of regularity. There might even be an outdated but readable newspaper or two tucked in the letter pouch.

The appetite the traders created for whiskey was soon to be choked off by an angry Canadian government. But the second appetite they created was too great for any government to kill. Albertans had tasted communication, and they weren't prepared to do without it any more.

Finally, on July 1, 1871, the Canadian government gave in and opened Alberta's first post office at Fort Saskatchewan (north of Edmonton). Soon a network of post offices covered the west and the stagecoach and pony express had replaced the "whiskey" express forever.

Today, there's hardly a farm or ranch without a mailbox at the gate, or a city house without a slot in the door. And we even have parcel post and registered letters and money orders. And Toronto no longer has a monopoly on street letter boxes.

And if every now and then one of the letters you receive smells faintly of whiskey, don't let it bother you. It's just the ghost of an ill wind that blew us a little good.

* * * *

ROLL THE PRESSES . . .
"The great man of today in Canada is made up of one part achievement and nine parts printers' ink"—Bob Edwards.

* * * *

Hanging in the newsrooms of The Lethbridge Herald and The Edmonton Journal are certificates honoring the two newspapers as joint winners of the first Pulitzer Prize ever to be awarded outside the United States.

The award came for courage rather than fine writing. Given the history of journalism in Alberta, there may be some justice in that.

Alberta's pioneers were prepared to do without a lot of things: streetlighting, trolleys, running water, and all those other civilized frills.

And they were patient, those early pioneers. Why, they waited 25 years for the mails to come here from the east, and then there was the telegraph and . . .

Well, doing-without and being patient has its limits. And by 1880 Albertans had decided they'd waited more than long enough for one essential of civilized life: the newspaper.

The call was out, and before they knew what had hit them Albertans suddenly had newspapers. And more newspapers and more newspapers.

In fact, for a while it seemed that Alberta was going to have more newspapers than the constitution can stand. It seemed you couldn't open a tent-flap or the door of a box car without running smack into a printing press and a sweating, swearing publisher "bringing the news" to Alberta.

A good many of those self-made "publishers", of course, never stayed in business past their first editions. They lasted only until their first paper hit the muddy streets and the outraged eyes of their readers.

Fortunately, for every deadbeat there were ten dedicated journalists who had the vision to look ahead to the future, and the enterprise to work to become part of that future.

These pioneer newsmen were trying to bring legitimate journalism to a frontier. And, judging from some of the perils they faced, "trying" is the best word to describe the life of a pioneer publisher.

* * * *

A SERIOUS APHAIR . . .

Lost somewhere in history are the origin of the Rocky Mountain Cyclone and the name of the brave soul who published it. Which may be just as well.

Unlike some of his competitors, who were resorting to carving type from wooden blocks, this gentleman decided to go whole-hog and order a press and type from a supplier in the east.

As the lead article in the first (and only known) issue of the Cyclone demonstrates, he might have been better off if he'd stuck to whittling:

"We begin the publication ov the Cyclone with some phew diphiculties in the way. The type phounder phrom whom we bought the outphit phor this printing ophice phailed to supply any ephs or cays, and it will be phour or phive weex bephore we can get any. We have ordered the missing letters, and we will have to wait until they come. We don't lique the idea ov this variety ov spelling any better than our readers do, but mistax will happen in the best-regulated phamilies, and iph the c's, x's and q's hold out we shall ceep (sound the c hard) the Cyclone whirling, aphter a phasion, until the sorts arrive. It's no joque to us; it is a serious aphair."

* * * *

THE BIBLE AND THE BULLETIN . . .

The Edmonton Bulletin was Alberta's first real newspaper. And Frank Oliver was Alberta's first real publisher.

The paper blared into existence on December 6, 1880, with the slogan "Read The Bible And The Bulletin." To a lot of p e o p l e — particularly in Edmonton — the slogan made sense.

Frank Oliver, after all, was something most other publishers of the time were not, a professional newspaperman. Even though he'd arrived in Edmonton to go into the grocery business, he'd first learned the newspaper trade working for the Winnipeg Free Press.

With credentials like that, it's easy to see why the people of Edmonton were willing to accept the Bulletin's slogan.

Credentials or not, it appears likely that Oliver would never have started the Bulletin had it not been for a want ad and a telegrapher with writer's cramp.

The advertisement was in Oliver's old paper, the Winnipeg Free Press, and pointed out that someone in Philadelphia had a printing press for sale for $20.

The writer's cramp belonged to Edmonton's over-worked telegrapher, Alec Taylor.

Taylor, for a long time, was the town's only source of news. So anxious were people for news of the rest of the world that Taylor used to write out, in long-hand, anything interesting that came over the wire and leave the bulletins on the counter of Frank Oliver's grocery store for the public to read.

Taylor was getting tired of the task, and the story goes that while he was delivering his bundle of telegraph news to Oliver's store one day, he spotted the advertisement in the Free Press.

"You worked on the Free Press, didn't you Frank?" he prodded Oliver. "If you know all about running a newspaper why don't you buy this press and start a paper? I'll give you all the news and I won't have to write it out myself."

Oliver was hesitantly considering the idea when Donald Ross, owner of the Edmonton Hotel, walked in. Taylor told him of the idea he was trying to sell Oliver, and Ross was so taken with it, he offered one of his hotel outbuildings as a place to set up the press — free.

With offers of free news and a free building, how could Oliver refuse?

So, in a matter of days, the Philadelphia press was westbound in a loaded freighter wagon.

At that time, the road to Edmonton involved a neverending series of fords across the Saskatchewan River. No sooner would a traveller come dripping out of the Saskatchewan on one side than he'd go splashing into it again on the other.

On one of these crossings, the wagon carrying Oliver's press tipped over and dumped all the large type into the water. It was never retrieved.

The loss would have been enough to stop Oliver had it not been for the determined telegrapher, Alec Taylor. Taylor was so anxious to have the paper come out that he personally carved, from blocks of wood, the large letters to form the words "THE BULLETIN", and Oliver went to press.

Frank Oliver, later, often said that those first editions were probably the smallest paper ever published. The Bulletin measured five inches wide by six inches deep (smaller than the page you're looking at!) and consisted of only four pages of printing when unfolded.

Alec Taylor, you'll recall, had promised Oliver free telegraph news. But, as luck would have it, the first issue of The Bulletin came out with its main headline reading: "No Telegrams."

The line had gone out the day before, and all Taylor's carving talent couldn't change that.

By the next week, however, the telegraph line was repaired and The Bulletin was in business. The paper was heady reading as a few samples from its first decade demonstrate:

—"George Gagnon lately killed a very large wolf, which, after disposing of one of his sheep, came back for another."

—"A Big Lake resident wants to know why the government potato contract was not awarded to him, seeing that his offer was 20 cents lower than that of the party who secured it."

—"Mr. Lucas, Government farmer at Peace Hills, has been supplied with his share of that band of cows. They are reported to be the sickest looking lot of animals in the county."

—"In New York City fully one half of the stage and cab horses are laid up with the epizootic."

—"Last Saturday morning the thermometers at Forts Edmonton and Saskatchewan registered 47 below zero."

Oliver's heart, however, was never really in the newspaper business. His real love was politics, particularly Liberal Party politics. In 1883, he won a seat on the North West Council. From then, until his death in 1933, Oliver was a politician first and a newspaper publisher only incidentally.

Despite the neglect, Liberal backing kept The Bulletin thriving for many years. It was only when the Liberals faded as a political force in Alberta in the 1930's that the paper began to suffer.

It struggled on until 1950, then quietly gave up and sold out to The Edmonton Journal.

If it died unhappily, The Bulletin could be proud that it had lived well. It had carried a city into the 20th Century. And, we mustn't forget, it also cured Edmonton's first telegrapher of what could have been the worst case of writer's cramp in Edmonton history.

* * * *

NOW AS I SEE IT . . .

Alberta's pioneer publishers had opinions on everything under the sun, and they considered it their divinely-inspired duty to share those opinions with their readers.

As a result, the pioneer newspaper seldom had an editorial page as we know it. It didn't need one. The whole paper was usually one long — and often outrageous — editorial.

That reader reaction often brought the not-so-delicate scent of bubbling tar and feathers wafting by the press-room door didn't seem to deter these pioneer journalists a bit.

Indeed, so taken were they with the approach, that Alberta newspapers remained largely organs of opinion until well into this century.

But as Bob Edwards (the opinionated publisher to end all opinionated publishers) p o i n t e d out, this brand of

journalism was, at best, a little risky. Writing in the Eye
Opener on June 6, 1902, he lamented:

It is simply impossible to run a paper without an oc-
casional error . . . As an example: "I've come," said the
visitor with the club, "to see why you called me a political
jobber in your paper today."

"I regret the error of the printer quite as much as you,"
replied the editor after opening a little drawer and taking
out a gun.

"Ah, then you didn't mean to call me that."

"No sir. I wrote robber very distinctly."

* * * *

NOW THERE WAS A MAN . . .

Studying the microfilmed collection of the Eye Opener in
the library of The Calgary Herald, a researcher felt someone at his shoulder and turned around to face a misty-eyed
oldtimer.

"Ah, the Eye Opener," the oldtimer blinked. "Now there was a paper.

"And Bob Edwards. Now there was a man."

It would be hard to find an Albertan who'd disagree.

"The price of this paper is one dollar a year," Bob Edwards once remarked. "It ought to be five but we knock off four for irregularity."

The Eye Opener and its publisher were, indeed, irregular. But more than anything or anyone else they managed to put Alberta — and Calgary in particular — on the map of the world.

Drunk or sober, this Scot with the soft heart and the sharp pen managed to produce a newspaper guaranteed to provoke both laughter and indignation — with more of the former than the latter. And if he created an international incident while he was at it, or tore a strip from some shady politician's back, or took a jab at the Canadian Pacific Railway, so much the better as far as he and most of his readers were concerned.

"One reason the Eye Opener has so many high ideals," he once suggested, "is that Calgary is over 3,000 feet above the level of the sea."

Bob Edwards did have his detractors. Not everyone appreciated his wit and that, combined with his perpetual lack of funds, forced him to move his paper from town to town until finally, in 1904, he and Calgary discovered one another and began an affair that lasted until his death in 1922.

The story of Bob Edwards deserves a whole book (like Eye Opener Bob by Grant MacEwan), and it would be an injustice to try to tell his story in these few pages.

Instead, we'd like to offer a sample of the Eye Opener itself. Although it lacks an example of Edwards' letters from that fictitious remittance man, Albert Buzzard-Cholomondeley of Skookingham, Leicestershire, England, what follows is a pretty fair taste of the famous weekly's front pages.

Indeed, apart from some deletions made for space reasons, it is exactly the front page that faced his Calgary readers when they unfolded their Eye Opener on August 18, 1906:

EYEOPENERS...

Cheer up! Only 18 more weeks of the present council.

Over in Riverside last week, amongst the Germans, a very pretty wedding was solemnized between Max Kahn the talented carpenter, and Miss Lena Katz. Considerable beer was licked up by the guests and the function, which otherwise would have passed off with great eclat, broke up in a free fight owing to a flippant remark made by someone present that the wedding seemed to him to be a case of catch as Katz Kahn.

It must make Lord's Day Alliance Shearer (who was no doubt immensely tickled at being invited by the cabinet to assist in framing the Lord's Day Bill) very sick at heart when he reads the Bill all over again in the quiet of his study. Instead of turning out, as the reverend gentleman and his long-faced friends fondly hoped, to be a compulsory insistence on the old Puritan Sunday of the well known Mayflower brand, the poor Bill got so changed around, amended, bent, twisted, and banged about by the wicked men in the House that it is now but a ghost of its former self.

The situation so far as actual Sunday observance goes is not changed to any annoying extent.

If passed as first proposed, it would have been an infringement of the liberty of the subject such as the public, as a mass, would not have stood for a moment. But the Bill was happily juggled about and broadened out at the last minute when nobody was looking. One of the amiable peculiarities of the act is that its real meanings are in the nature of connundrums which, because it would cost a lot to try them out by legal process, will probably remain puzzles forever.

The act prohibits all manner of participation in any game, performance or meeting held for gain, or from which there are "gate receipts", except at church doors. Amateur golf, cricket, baseball, polo, footracing, or theatricals, on Sunday are permitted. Think of that, ye soreheads who have been kicking about the Lord's Day Act! The Lord's Day Act is all right, in spots.

As to working on the Sawbath. You can do any work of necessity and mercy on the Sawbath. Such works are specified, and include telegraph and telephone service, c a r r y i n g travellers, renting and hiring carriages and small boats, preparing M o n d a y morning newspapers, and, generally speaking, pretty much every sort of work that will not make capital lose some profit nor labor some employment.

Nothing the matter with that, is there?

Radcliffe, our genial hangman, has applied to the government for leave to augment his s a l a r y by travelling with a circus and giving exhibitions of his skill. If the permission is granted, which we v e r y much doubt, Mr. Radcliffe proposes to "put on" Burchell's execution in all its detail, a cleverly prepared dummy of the f a m o u s murderer h a v i n g already been secured from a well known Woodstock taxidermist. It is likely, also, that he may strive to amuse the children who stay for the concert with a comic representation of how he choked off a couple of Chinamen at Nanaimo last year.

In t h i s connection, we might be permitted to suggest that Radcliffe be given the appointment of Official Foolkiller at a fair remuneration, his duties being to respond to calls from such towns as require his services. The only drawback to this suggestion is that he might, in order to save himself endless journeyings to and fro, decide to change his place of residence f r o m Toronto to Calgary.

Do read the following astonishing incident which occurred at Olds (Cloakeyville) the other day.

It didn't occur exactly at Olds, but a lake four or five miles from town, where they have picnics, pleasure parties, and so forth.

T h r e e Olds gentlemen were out for a sail in a boat. It was a very nice boat, but it had no keel. Consequently the sail had to be manipulated with the greatest care and skill.

Well, to make a long story short, a gust of wind struck the boat when about a quarter of a mile from shore and over she went. The three men floundered about in the water which was fifteen feet deep, and great was the panic and excitement among the pleasure-seekers picnicking along the beach.

A young Scots sectionhand named Brown, a splendid swimmer, doft all his clothes to the buff and swam out to the rescue.

Another boat reached the drowners about the same time as he did, and pulled them aboard. Scotty Brown, however, decided to swim back.

When he reached t h e shore there was quite a crowd of ladies and gentlemen waiting for the rescued party. Among them was the wife of one of the men who were upset, a couple of school-mamms, and several others of the fair sex.

Scotty landed without a stitch of clothes on him, but the crowd was too much engrossed over the partially drowned men to pay very much attention to him. However, it appears that he did not go entirely unnoticed for, later on, one of the ladies was heard to exclaim in tones of intense admiration, "Well, I'll say this for Mr. Brown. He showed us he was a man anyhow!"

A newspaper has been started at the flourishing town of Midnapore, nine miles south of Calgary. It is called the Midnapore Gazette and is edited by a gentleman whose writings will never be mistaken for those of Mr. Goldwin Smith. One of the locals reads— "Mrs. Jimmy O s b o r n e, wife of our talented butcher, fell down the cellar steps last Tuesday and broke her knee-cap. The Gazette extends its sympathy to Mrs. Osborne in this her hour of bereavement."

The M.P.P.'s excursion appears to have been but a dreary affair. When will people who get up excursions intended specially for the amusement or instruction of a body of men engaged in some particular line of business, when will they tumble to the fact that any such excursion which includes "the women-folk" is bound to be a frost?

We never knew it fail yet. The wives and daughters act as a veritable wet blanket over the whole proceedings and effectively put a stopper on any fun and hilarity that might otherwise be indulged in by the men who are supposed to be off on a holiday.

The men are afraid to take a drink or to hit 'er up and strike a gait. If somebody starts to sing, the ladies conclude he is drunk. Poker is sidetracked, as is a l s o the interchange of stories.

Then, again, ladies are prone to criticize. "Mr. So and So is such a charming man, while Mr. Toodleupteday is such a horrid man"— "Don't you think Mr. Joskins might dress a little better?" —"Where did Mr. McGonigle pick up that awful wife of his?"—"I think it very bad taste for the men to be always around the dining car conductor t a k i n g drinks when ladies are along." and so forth and so forth.

No, no! The Lord preserve us from an excursion where "the women-folk" are along. We have been there.

From all we can learn of the M.P.P.'s excursion it seems to have been a kind of juggernaut business from start to finish, the triumphant Liberals rolling in uncanny majesty over the hapless country crushing all Conservatives foolish enough to get in their path.

The two hapless members of the opposition, Robertson, and Don Hiebert were ignored most shabbily, neither being invited to speak nor even to show themselves as curiosities. This was all in exceedingly poor taste.

Nor was Mr. Young of the Herald, though a guest, invited to warble for the press. This was reserved for the great Liberal orator, Duncan Marshall, than whom there is no more fascinating talker in the west.

Liberalism was riotously triumphant. It was a grand missionary trip for the party, fall wheat and beet sugar being of secondary consideration.

Robertson and Don Hiebert should make the trip all over again by themselves and raise hell generally on behalf of the badly chewed-up Conservative party.

Let us draw a long breath and wait for the first despatch from London announcing Frank Oliver's presentation to King Edward. His Majesty will no doubt be grief-stricken when he learns that Callahan has broken out of the new Edmonton jail.

After the next municipal election some of the present aldermen will put in an interesting half hour wondering why they ever took the trouble to stand as candidates again.

We heard a pretty good yarn the other day, happily free from all suggestion of double entendre, as so many good yarns are not—. It is about a visit to a sick bed.

Before being allowed to enter the chamber to have a chat with his sick friend, who was of a very stubborn, contumacious nature, he was handed the usual line of warning about cheering the odd fellow up and making light of his illness and so forth.

"Well, well, old chap," he cried cheerily to the patient, "you're looking fine. I don't believe you're sick at all."

"Me not sick! Great Scot! I'm awful sick."

"Not a bit of it, not a bit of it! Only imagination my dear boy. You are looking ever so much better since I was here."

"You are a liar."

"Why, old fellow, you are, upon my word! Eyes bright, good color, cheerful demen—"

"What are you giving me you blasted idiot! I tell you I am much worse."

"Oh nonsense!"

"Damned your eyes, I am!"

"Oh, pshaw!"

"Look here you fool, you chuckling head, you—you busted record. Look here! You see me lying here on the flat of my back! Well, the doctor tells me, and he is corroborated by four others, that if I turn over on my side I am a dead man."

"I don't believe a word of it my dear sir."

"You call me a liar?"

"Well, not exactly—"

"By God I'll show you!" roared the exasperated patient. And with that the old codger, to prove his point, deliberately rolled over on his side and was dead inside of a minute. One last few seconds being devoted to a significant movement of his arm, as much as to say, "What did I tell you?"

* * * *

It is easy to see why Bob Edward's readers looked forward so impatiently to every issue of the Eye Opener.

Edwards was rarely really vindictive. And even when he was being particularly "down" on someone, his wit had a way of making the victim grin while he squirmed. As in the following example from the Eye Opener while it was being published in High River in 1903:

"We read in A Book of Curious Facts that a pair of hogs owned 10 years have a progeny of 6,634,838 pigs, and yet Mike Moran and Peter McDermott, two talented citizens who are too fly for their own good, have each been married for a longer period than that and have only two children apiece. According to the above, they ought to have 6,634,838."

* * * *

While Bob Edwards could fire his barbs into largely willing hides, most other Alberta publishers could not. Lacking Edwards' wit and wisdom, some newspaper owners turned the power of their presses loose in shrill, cruel and discriminatory attacks on those who couldn't fight back.

Anyone wanting to see the results of these kinds of attacks should find a copy of the Innesvale Freelance of Feb. 8, 1900.

There is hardly an item on the first page of that issue that can be reprinted. Certainly there is hardly an item that wouldn't land an editor in court on a libel or defamation charge if he dared to print it today.

This kind of mud-slinging journalism, combined with the newspapers' increasing interference in politics didn't take long to stir discontent among Alberta readers — and to draw the stern eye of political leaders. It wouldn't be too many years before this discontent and political disapproval took their toll.

* * * *

LET'S DILLY DAILY . . .

For a long time Alberta was weekly newspaper country. It was hard enough to get out a paper once a week — what with rooting out advertisers and getting deliveries to subscribers — without trying the nightmare existence of daily publication.

But, inevitably, there were men among those early publishers who were bold enough and farsighted enough to see that Alberta's growing towns were ripe markets for daily papers.

The first to make the leap and survive was The Calgary Herald. Founded as a weekly on August 31, 1883 under the name "The Calgary Weekly Herald, Mining and Ranch Advocate," The Herald went daily on July 2, 1885 and has been at it ever since.

As other towns grew large enough to support the move, more and more papers followed the trend to daily publication.

Gradually, as the 1900's passed into their teens, then their twenties and thirties, Alberta's newspapers changed and began to look more and more the way they look today. But, in one important way, they didn't change quickly enough.

* * * *

FREEDOM OF THE PRESS . . .

The press tradition of freedom of opinion wasn't unique to Alberta. But, with the possible exception of some of the newspapers of the American southwest, nowhere was that tradition practised more fervently.

Today, the Alberta newspaper is careful to bundle most of its opinions onto one page under the warning label "Editorials." And, today, Alberta newspapers are careful not to let their political views color news reporting.

But, until well into the 1920's, that was seldom the case. Anyone — especially politicians — were fair game for any kind of verbal attack. And many people — especially the smarting politicians — were beginning to feel the time was ripe to bring Alberta's newspapers into line.

The move to control the press came in 1937. And — as is so often the way — when it was made, it was made at the wrong time and in the wrong way.

By 1937, Alberta's newspapers, growing in size and in conscience, had already made the shift to "responsible" journalism.

But in 1937 there was a new political party in Alberta, the Social C r e d i t Party, and it had won control of the government two years earlier. Like all new parties — particularly when they find themselves running a government — this one felt a little insecure.

And there's nothing like the prospect of a hostile press to turn insecurity into reaction.

The attack started, not against one of the giants like The Edmonton Journal or The Calgary Herald, but against the small and quiet-spoken Lethbridge Herald.

The headline jolted every publisher in the province:

"Herald's Press Gallery Correspondent Threatened with Expulsion from House: Refuses to Reveal Sources of News."

The story The Lethbridge Herald ran under that headline made it plain what kind of war was coming:

EDMONTON — What may rightly be regarded as the big stick hangs over the veteran head of the Herald's legislative correspondent in the press gallery.

The Herald on several occasions has had stories some days in advance of the other daily newspapers on steps being considered by government and caucus for taxation, debt adjustment and other matters of policy. Prior to making his second budget speech in the House Friday afternoon, Provincial Treasurer Solon Low called the Herald correspondent to his office, where Chairman Glen MacLachlan and Commissioner L. D. Byrne of the Social Credit Board, and A. J. Hooke, government whip, were gathered. Mr. Low asked the correspondent where he obtained information for all the wild stories.

Recently, in caucus, it is reported, Hon. Mr. Low raised the same question and is said to have suggested a ruling that the Herald correspondent be denied the privilege of the press gallery. This the caucus declined to do.

At Friday's grilling, Mr. Low admitted there was a "kernel of truth" in the stories but insisted they were not in accord with the facts. The correspondent . . . flatly refused to divulge the source of such information . . . Mr. Low threatened expulsion from the press gallery might follow a repetition of the policy on the part of the correspondent, who replied that this was entirely up to Mr. Low.

* * * *

If anyone thought the incident just another political squabble, they were soon to learn differently.

Premier William Aberhart, only weeks later, was quoted in The Edmonton Journal as advocating licensing of newspapers and attacking the handling of news by the "so-called free press", charging they heeded the dictates of the "money barons" with r e s u l t a n t "false colouring" of dispatches.

What the government hopefully considered the final solution to the problem of the "so-called free press" was passage of a piece of legislation innocently titled: "An Act to Ensure the Publication of Accurate Information."

The act placed control of newspaper space under the Social Credit Board. It required publishers, d a i l y and weekly, to print the objects and policies of the government. And it decreed that a publisher must reveal the source by name and address of all information published and the identity of the writer of any editorial, article or news item.

Heavy penalties were provided; among other things, the suspension of any offending newspaper, and the outlawing of any newspaperman the Social Credit Board might specify.

The act touched off a furor that filled editorial pages from coast to coast.

In retrospect, one of the worst mistakes the government made was in opening its attack against The Lethbridge Herald.

The Herald might be small and quiet-spoken, but its publisher, W. A. Buchanan, was one of the toughest, most dedicated newspapermen in Canada.

Ontario-born, Buchanan had learned the newspaper business from the press-room up. He could set type, run a press, write a story, and do literally every job involved in newspaper production. He'd come west in search of a newspaper of his own; a newspaper he could run freely and well.

Buying in as a partner in the weekly Herald, he soon owned it outright, and not much later boldly moved it to daily status.

The legislation to control the press violated every principle he held, and he was out to fight it to the bitter end.

It was Buchanan, backed by John M. Imrie of The Edmonton Journal and F. P. Galbraith of The Red Deer Advocate, who was chosen by Alberta's newsmen to fight the act to defeat.

Actually, the controversial act was already in trouble. Before it could become law, it had to have Royal assent, the signature of Lieutenant-Governor Bowlen. Instead of signing, Bowlen sat on the bill for a while then — as was his constitutional right — handed it over to the Governor-General in Council at Ottawa for a decision.

The federal government, in turn, referred the bill to the Supreme Court of Canada for a ruling on its "constitutionality."

Before the Supreme Court, in N o v e m b e r, 1937, Buchanan fought the case for the Alberta publishers. Three months later, the court ruled the act ultra vires — and the Judicial Committee of the Privy Council in London backed the ruling.

The press bill was dead.

A year later, from New York, came a footnote that began:

THE TRUSTEES OF COLUMBIA UNIVERSITY

IN THE CITY OF NEW YORK

To All Persons to Whom

these Presents May Come Greetings

Be it known that

THE LETHBRIDGE HERALD

Has been Awarded Recognition with the EDMONTON JOURNAL, recipient of a special Pulitzer Prize for Distinguished and Meritous Public Service in 1937. In accordance with the provisions of . . .

It was Alberta Journalism's proudest moment.

* * * *

ORDINARY GARDEN VARIETY . . .

Looking over Alberta's newspapers today, some people — particularly oldtimers — are inclined to grumble that they "ain't like they used to be."

In some ways, they're right. But, in other ways, they're wrong.

True, it's only Fred Kennedy of The Albertan who makes the old-time claim that "I write as I please" and sticks to it (to the amusement and indignation of thousands of devoted readers).

But personal opinion was never really the mainstay of our newspapers. It was always the people of Alberta themselves. And the tradition of the people's newspaper is very much alive and growing, particularly among our weeklies.

The "typical" Alberta publisher today is very much like Neil Leatherdale of the Olds Gazette who points out proudly that his policy of printing "ordinary garden variety

news" has raised his circulation in the 26 years he has run the paper from 1,200 to 5,000

Leaning back in a swivel chair in his crowded print shop, Mr. Leatherdale grumbles cheerfully that too many Alberta papers are "trying to get too darn sophisticated," instead of giving readers what they really want —news about themselves.

One of his proudest claims, and one that may point to the success of rural weeklies, is that his newspaper is mostly written by the people who read it.

"About 65 to 70 per cent of our material is sent in by people who want material published. We try to stick to what they say.

"If people have taken the time to write it, then my obligation is to take the time to read it, make sure it's understandable, and then make sure my boys set it in type the way they sent it in."

As far as Mr. Leatherdale is concerned, every Alberta newspaper is political. They always have been and they always will be. Personally — and most newsmen echo his feelings — he believes that there is nothing wrong in being political as long as you're honest about it, and as long as you're fair.

"I'm a Liberal and I make no bones about it. But at the same time I try to be fair. I think you have to. I don't think there's such a thing as being independent. I don't think this is possible.

"And, therefore, anybody who says they're independent is just kidding themselves.

"Everybody knows what my politics are, but, at the same time, I try to be fair about them. If a guy has done a good job, I'm willing to say that he's done a good job. And I think that's the most important part of the whole newspaper business today.

"Don't beat the bush just for the sake of beating the bush.

"Of course," he adds with a Bob Edwards' glitter in his eye, "it doesn't hurt to have a sense of humor, too."

* * * *

When a newspaper writer reaches the bottom of a page in a continuing story, he closes the page with the word "more."

And maybe that's the best place to leave Alberta journalism right now. With Neil Leatherdale and the word "more."

* * * *

POUNDING BRASS . . .

It was January, 1879 and Albertans had been getting mail service for nearly three years and were only a year away from their first newspaper.

And in Edmonton, a handful of people shivered near the door of a building at the Hudson's Bay post to listen anxiously for a flurry of clicks and clacks that would tell them the age of modern communication had arrived.

They didn't have to wait long. First there was a short burst of clicking, then another, and finally a nervous Alec Taylor started "pounding brass" in reply. The telegraph had come to Edmonton, and the cluster of people outside the door had the satisfaction of knowing they'd finally "caught up" with that unluckiest of companies, Dominion Telegraph.

Why unluckiest of companies? Well, because Dominion Telegraph had committed that deadliest of corporate errors: it guessed wrong.

In 1876, the company had hastily thrown up a telegraph line along what it (and the rest of Canada) had been led to believe would be the route of the new Canadian Pacific Railway. With a railroad line as mainstay, argued Dominion's directors, how could a telegraph company lose?

It could lose, as time would prove, all too easily. All it takes is for the Canadian Pacific Railway to change its mind — and its route.

But in 1879, Dominion Telegraph and the cluster of people in Edmonton didn't know anything about all that. All they knew was that the telegraph line, faithfully following the CPR map, ran through the present town of Leduc — 20 miles south of Edmonton.

Indignant at being left out of the modern age by Dominion T e l e g r a p h, Edmonton residents had been petitioning the federal government since 1878 in a bid to get the company to run a line north.

Indignation had got them nowhere. In the end, Edmonton had to find itself a contractor willing to supply material free of charge, and then make a generous offer to defray the expense of running the line north. Then, and only then, did Dominion bring the telegraph to Edmonton.

So the victory the people were celebrating outside Alec Taylor's shack was a little hollow (particularly in the region of the pocket-book).

It would seem even hollower as time went by and the people of Edmonton discovered that telegraph service, as offered by Dominion, wasn't all it was cracked up to be.

At its best, Dominion Telegraph's service meant instant communication with the whole world. But it was seldom at its best, thanks to poor wire, prairie fires — and itchy buffalo.

The line stretched nearly 1,000 miles west from Winnipeg, and it was 1,000 miles of pure trouble.

Poles were poplar, a wood whose only virtue is the accuracy with which it can be predicted how quickly it will rot at ground level. Wire was of such poor quality that, during wet weather in wooded areas, the signal wouldn't carry more than a few miles.

Even when poles weren't rotting off or wire wasn't out, Dominion could always count on a prairie fire or two to warm things up for them.

And then there were the buffalo. As low as Dominion Telegraph might rate on anyone else's popularity poll, the buffalo had them right on top of the list for being good enough to provide them with a thousand miles of back-scratchers.

The buffalo rubbed Dominion's poles smooth. In some places, they rubbed them right through. And every few days a really enthusiastic bull was guaranteed to actually knock down a pole — or a whole string of poles.

Alberta's first telegraph service wasn't, to say the least, all it might have been.

* * * *

CHECKERS AND CHECK-UPS . . .

Dominion Telegraph may not have brought its customers the best service in the world. But, in spite of that, it did bring some profound changes to pioneer life.

For one thing, it did much to bring peace. The North-West Mounted Police had come west in 1874 as a small force, and they counted on the telegraph to call them to the scene of trouble in a hurry.

So effective was the telegraph in this capacity that potentially troublesome Indians began speaking fearfully of it as the "speaking iron", a particularly potent form of white magic.

On one occasion, when a band of Indians rode up to a telegraph station and began to make abusive demands for free provisions, the operator wired for help then stalled for time.

Troops were there the next morning and the Indians fled in terror, convinced the police had come over the wire.

The telegraph also brought health service to a frontier where physicians were rare, and injury and illness were common.

Dominion Telegraph always had a doctor on call to handle emergency appeals for medical advice, and charged nothing for the service. It was a rough and ready form of doctoring, usually, but it saved countless lives.

And the telegraph also brought an entertainment bonus Dominion Telegraph hadn't counted on when it built its line.

When part of the line was out — which was often the case — operators on "live" sections would turn over their telegraph keys to the frontier checker experts for long-distance games in Morse code. Edmonton, ever aggressive in sports, was always on the wire challenging all comers in Battleford and Qu'Appelle.

* * * *

THE DOOMED DOMINION . . .

Dominion Telegraph had built its line on the gamble that the CPR would follow the same route west. When the gamble didn't pay off, and CPR ran its rail far to the south, it was only a matter of time before Dominion would have to settle its gambling debts.

The principal day of reckoning came in 1886 when the CPR started its own telegraph system, much more efficient than Dominion's, to carry messages back and forth across all of Canada.

Dominion struggled on for nearly two decades longer, surviving by filling the gap in telegraph service in northern Alberta. But then came the final blow.

In the early 1900's the Grand Trunk Pacific Railway pushed north through the province with rail — and a modern telegraph system.

By the time Grand Trunk reached Edmonton, Dominion was finished. Business dwindled and dwindled until finally, like the buffalo no longer there to rub against their rotting poles, Dominion Telegraph quietly disappeared.

* * * *

THIS IS GOD SPEAKING . . .

It was Edmonton's Alec Taylor who persuaded Frank Oliver to start Alberta's first newspaper. It was Alec Taylor who served as Alberta's first telegrapher.

And it was the same Alec Taylor who started the first known telephone system in the province.

It wasn't, it must be pointed out right away, as big a project to start a telephone system in the 1880's as it would be today.

All it took was two sets, some wire, and a battery.

Like many others, Alec Taylor had read of Alexander Graham Bell's experiments with the telephone in 1874. And, like many others, Mr. Taylor was intrigued by the spread of telephone systems in the east.

When, in 1884, Mr. Taylor began to see advertisements in the periodicals touting an English-made telephone, he broke down and ordered two sets.

With the encouragement of the Hudson's Bay factor, Mr. Taylor ran a line between his telegraph office and the Hudson's Bay post. The idea was to cut out all the tiresome running back and forth with telegraph messages, and it almost worked out that way.

Early telephones were eccentric creatures at best, especially operating on lines as makeshift as the one between the telegraph office and Hudson's Bay post. At best it took a lot of yelling and hallooing — and a little cursing — to get the faintest of messages through. At worst, well, it was back to hand-delivering all those telegrams.

If the first two phones weren't too successful in the business field, Mr. Taylor did manage to put them to good use to solve an annoying personal problem.

Every day, punctually, as Mr. Taylor would open his telegraph office, an old Indian would shuffle in, squat down by the stove, and sit smoking until closing time. Alec Taylor tolerated the daily invasion for a long time, but he finally got fed up.

One day he arranged for a friend to come to the office, then hurried down to the Bay post. From there he telephoned back and had the friend call the Indian to the phone.

The Indian was horrified to hear an awesome, crackling voice address him with the message:

"This is God speaking. I want you to get out of that office and stay out!"

Mr. Taylor's office was Indian-free from that day forward.

* * * *

HELLO, OPERATOR? OPERATOR? . . .

Alec Taylor soon discovered that anyone in Edmonton with two telephones was in the telephone business — whether he wanted to be or not.

Slowly, lines spread from his office to service new customers, and by 1886 Alec Taylor had installed a switchboard — and a pretty, young lady to operate it.

Jane Lauder, later to become the wife of Sen. Griesbach, was Edmonton's — and Alberta's — first telephone operator. And she soon had, as Edmonton historian Naomi Radford points out, "all Edmonton at her fingertips."

There was nothing impersonal about Miss Jane's service. There couldn't be. Nearly every caller was a relative or a friend, and requests for information were made on a personal level.

"Janie dear, find Dr. Wilson for me, will you?" or "I want that little German butcher woman, please," were the forms the requests took. Naturally, Jane Lauder — with only 20 telephones on the line — was notably successful in tracking down the elusive Dr. Wilson, and in connecting callers to the happy, guttural voice of the proprietress of the meat store.

Thinking of Janie, one can't help but wonder what the reaction would be today if you asked the impersonal voice of the telephone operator to connect you with "that little German butcher lady, please."

* * * *

LONG DISTANCE, PLEASE . . .

Not content with all his other "firsts", Alec Taylor took it upon himself to arrange what seems to have been the west's first long-distance telephone call.

It was soon after Mr. Taylor's first two phones were hooked up, and there was a widespread debate taking place about the possibility or impossibility of long-distance voice communication.

Mr. Taylor said it could be done, and virtually everyone else in Edmonton said it couldn't.

So Mr. Taylor said somewhat heatedly that not only could it be done but he'd "d—n well prove it."

Taylor, as telegraph operator, had a thousand miles of wire at his disposal. He arranged for a cohort at Battleford to hook a telephone set onto the line there, and he did the same himself at Edmonton.

One midnight, with all the telegraph stations between the two points shut down, Taylor and his opposite in Battleford each cranked up tiny hand-operated generators and began making futile attempts to ring one another.

The little generators, however, weren't strong enough. But after three or four minutes, both men conceived the idea of screaming "hello" into the set, and made contact.

For 10 or 15 minutes — long enough to settle the sceptics — the two succeeded in making one another understand a few phrases.

Having settled the hash of those who had disagreed with him, Taylor promptly turned his back on the whole issue of long-distance and returned to his perennial problem of trying to make contact with the Hudson's Bay post a few blocks away.

It wasn't until 1891 that the first true long-distance line in the province was installed between Cardston and Lethbridge. Unfortunately, according to contemporary reports, it spent most of its time being out of service.

* * * *

A LITTLE CHAOS . . .

For a while after Edmonton started up the telephone bandwagon, every town in the province was hopping on and off; installing switchboards and tearing them out again, putting up lines and taking down lines.

In Calgary, where the city fathers had taken the precaution of calling in the Bell Telephone Company to install their system in 1887, service was so bad that the city's 40 customers refused to pay their bills.

* * * *

A WORD FROM THE CUCKOO . . .

Rural service, started by the Edmonton District Telephone Company in 1904, proved even more of a headache than city service.

It seems that some rural customers took quite a shine to the idea of eavesdropping on other people's calls — "rubbering in" as the practice was known.

In fact, it seems that so many rural customers liked to rubber-in that transmission often just gave out from the strain of having all those phones on the line at once.

The telephone company, naturally, took a dim view of the practice — threatening legal action and worse. But, of course, as customers knew all too well, it's a lot easier to threaten action than to take it in the case of so elusive a culprit as an eavesdropper.

In fact, the only recorded case of the company catching up with anyone was that of an unhappy gentleman who had the bad luck to own the only cuckoo clock in the district. And who had the misfortune to have his cuckoo clock "cuckoo" when he just happened to be listening in on a call.

* * * *

A CALL FROM THE LEGISLATURE . . .

Finally, in 1906, Alberta's government took a look at the world of telephone service and decided that it was just too chaotic.

There wasn't enough service to meet the mushrooming demands of the population, and what service there was spent most of its time out of order.

Alec Taylor had already sold out his Edmonton system to the city and wiped his hands of the whole business. Other private operators were doing the same in other towns.

So the legislature, pressed by private members, voted

$25,000 "for the purpose of investigating the advisability of government-owned telephones."

Two years later, Alberta Government Telephones was in business with the promise to "have a telephone system of its own connecting every part of this province, not only the towns, villages and cities of Alberta but also the rural portions where telephone communication is practicable and where the people desire to have it."

It is a promise that AGT, with more than half a million phones in service today, has kept singularly well. Even if the operator doesn't know who you mean by "that little German butcher lady."

* * * *

AND THIS IS CHBC, CALGARY . . .

Albertans, moving into the 1920's, had lost most of their sense of isolation.

After all, regular mail delivery was almost half a century old, telegraph lines criss-crossed the province, most homes had a telephone. What more could anyone want?

Well, there was this new-fangled something called radio. Not too many people in Alberta had actually heard a radio, but the newspapers were full of it and it seemed to be catching on like wildfire in the east and in the states. It would be nice, some people felt, to have a radio to listen to on those long winter nights.

By 1921, the Dominion air board had established a research station at High River, and an engineer named W. W. Grant was busy holding two-way radio conversations with other engineers in places like Denver, Colorado.

Then, in May, 1922, Mr. Grant came to Calgary and, with the backing of The Morning Albertan, brought CHBC to the airways. It was Alberta's first radio station.

By May, 1923, the Albertan could report:

"One year ago this week, CHBC, the radiophone broadcasting station of The Morning Albertan, officially commenced broadcasting concerts and news bulletins. Today, The Morning Albertan station, through its marvelous achievements, notably in long distance broadcasting, is known the continent over as one of the most powerful in the United States and Canada. In every city in every state in the United States and Canada, The Albertan station is known."

A little heavy on self-praise, perhaps, but true.

All over the province, people were plugging into crystal sets, and every businessman who could dig up a transmitter and an engineer was getting into the act.

* * * *

"BOMBING" IN EDMONTON . . .

Edmonton may have been a whisper short of beating its rival city to the south onto the air, but what it lacked in speed, it made up for in quantity. It soon had three stations running. To the confusion of listeners, all three ran on the same frequency.

Powerful U.S. stations were already plugging most available frequencies, and the few Canadian stations with high-powered transmitters had snatched up most of the rest. Edmonton had to be satisfied with the dregs.

Having three radio stations on the same frequency wasn't as confusing as it might seem. Radio in the 1920's was still very heavy on silence, broadcasting only a few hours a day. So it wasn't hard to work out a sharing arrangement.

Inevitably, of course, this "arrangement" led to a few mistakes. Like the night The Bible Students station,

CHCY, and the Journal station, CJCA, came on the air at the same time.

The combination of "Yes, Sir, That's My Baby" and divine prayer must have done strange things to listeners' ears and minds.

Edmonton, of course, also had to be more eccentric than Calgary.

In CJCA, for example, the announcer had to go off the air when he wanted to open a window, because the station's high-voltage cables ran across the studio window.

So, naturally, one night owner-announcer Dick Rice went to open the window. And, naturally, he didn't turn off the power. And, naturally, he was promptly knocked unconscious.

Rival station CHCY, equally exciting, recaptured the airwaves with a bomb scare.

Their transmitter was out in the wilderness, right in the middle of the present subdivision of Idylwylde. One Saturday night, an anonymous telephone tip warned the station control room that the transmitter was marked for a dynamite plot.

Technicians and friends rushed to the scene and found an appropriately ticking parcel. Frantic, they dumped the parcel in a pail of water until the ticking stopped. Then they opened it.

Inside was a clock wired to four batteries which, in turn, was wired to four giant firecrackers. It didn't turn out to be a complete fizzle, however. One of the firecrackers managed to go off with a loud roar.

It caused, one of those present recalled later, "a great amount of excitement."

* * * *

THE ELECTRONIC LECTURER...

The most frustrated man in Alberta radio had to be H. P. Brown, in charge of the visual aid department at the University of Alberta. And that's because, try as he might, he wasn't in Alberta radio.

As early as 1921, Mr. Brown was making earnest attempts to get U. of A. to set up an educational radio station. No luck.

Mr. Brown begged and pleaded, then begged and pleaded some more. But the university stood adamant. No radio for the University of Alberta.

Now, Mr. Brown was a persistent man. And a patient one. And he wasn't above using a little trickery to get what he wanted.

Somehow, the 1927 budget for the university contained, at Mr. Brown's instigation, $7,000 for a new lecturer in the department of extension.

Several months passed without anyone noticing that the new lecturer hadn't arrived on the scene — and without anyone becoming suspicious of an unusual amount of activity among electrical engineering students.

No one, unbelievably, even particularly noticed that the department of extension had graced the campus with two old windmill towers, 75 feet high, and topped with iron rods stretching up another 25 feet! (They stood around until 1966, by the way.)

All that took a powerful lot of not noticing.

By the time anyone did notice, it was too late. The "new lecturer" had turned into $2,000 worth of radio station, and CKUA was an accomplished fact. The patient Mr. Brown was the first announcer. Which just shows that you can't keep a determined man shut up forever.

* * * *

WITH A LOAN AND A LITTLE "LOVE" . . .

With the possible exception of Edmonton's Dick Rice, no man has played a larger role in Alberta broadcasting history than H. Gordon Love of Calgary.

Strangely enough, he got into the broadcasting business through the wrong end — by wanting to sell radios. In

1922, he and a partner started the Radio Corporation of Calgary as the sales outlet for an eastern radio manufacturer.

It didn't take the pair long to discover that they were going to have a powerful hard time selling radios to people unless there was something to hear on the radios. So the two approached The Calgary Herald and made a deal to erect a 500 watt station, CFAC, on top of the Herald building. The transmitter was in a small shack by the tower.

Love didn't stay stuck on top of the Herald building for long, however. Within a few years he had purchased the ailing CFCN and left radio sales behind forever.

By 1931, after bouncing from location to location in the city. Love put up a 10,000 watt transmitter at Strathmore and staked CFCN's claim as "The Voice of The Prairies," a claim that has never been relinquished.

He recalls those early years, when he was getting started, as tough ones — filled with bitter competition between radio and newspaper.

"At the time I started commercial radio broadcasting, Col. Wood at The Herald had every businessman on 8th Ave. owing him just enough money so they couldn't write a cheque for it.

"If any commercial was placed with us and Wood heard it, he would phone the advertiser and say: We've been real good to you, right? If the man didn't get the message, Wood would demand his money and the guy would have to cancel his commercials.

"Many times I had to lend guys money to pay off Wood just to stay on the air."

Under Gordon Love's direction, CFCN recorded a lot of "firsts", but none that makes him prouder than the fact

CFCN provided the first independent news service in Canada, in 1935.

The news came in by wireless from New York and was taken down, first by hand, then by typewriter. At one point it came in over a receiver in north Calgary and was rushed to the station by bicycle.

The west's first recreated sports broadcasts — of a World Series game in St. Louis — was sent over the airwaves by CFCN, with Gordon Love handling the broadcast himself.

Mr. Love, who had played professional baseball himself, called the game from dispatches that came in by telegraph and were handed to him while he was on the air.

He recalls with some amusement that, getting caught up in the game, he became quite liberal with description and atmosphere — provided solely by his imagination.

But, as it turned out, his imagination was in perfect working order. At one point in the broadcast, he told his listeners — purely on guesswork — that Babe Ruth had hit the ball right out of the catcher's hand.

"Later on," he grins, "a picture of that game came out and, sure enough, there was Ruth doing it just the way I described it."

* * * *

EAR PLUGS, PLEASE ...

Most Albertans were enchanted with the arrival of radio. But not all. The Calgary Herald found room in its edition of Feb. 20, 1929, to express the quiet hope that new station, CJOC, would arrange its programs so that "radio fans will turn the dials for the local station and be able to hear interesting arrangements and that the use of phonograph records will be kept to a minimum."

On the same page, more pointedly, there was an "Otto Watt" cartoon that had Otto brooding over his bed and radio and muttering: "What to do, What to do." When a lady friend asked what was bothering him, he replied: "Oh I'm trying to decide which to get rid of — my bed or my radio. I don't need them both!"

* * * *

TRY THE HORIZONTAL HOLD . . .

If Otto Watt had been around in October, 1953, he'd really have had something to worry about. That was the month Alberta's first five television station licences were issued. Less than a year later, CFRN in Edmonton and CHCT in Calgary were on the air.

In the process of setting up, Calgary finally outdid Edmonton in the showmanship department. A month before CHCT was to go on the air, it managed to have its huge transmission tower fall over.

* * * *

THE SOUNDS OF SILENCE . . .

Today, in Alberta, communication — and the noise it makes — is everywhere. Where a hundred years ago people didn't really know what was happening a mile away, today they can see the whole world through the window of a television set.

Radios come in stereo and with ear plugs. Cars can be equipped with tape-decks. Newspapers can put out editions of more than 100 pages.

The old Morse key has been replaced with rattling tele-type and broadband and satellite transmission, and tele-phones ring incessantly.

It's enough to make some who remember pioneer days think of Bill Peyto, the famous Rocky Mountain guide. In-evitably, when Bill found himself stuck with a particularly noisy party in a mountain camp, he'd grab his bedroll and head over the hill muttering something about finding "a little durn peace and quiet."

Wait up, Bill.

POLITICS AND A PROMISE

"Politics has not ceased to make strange bedfellows; at least the politicians continue to share the same bunk. You know the kind of bunk we mean." — Bob Edwards.

* * * *

It's not that pioneer Albertans didn't take politics seriously. They did. But they always took it with a grain of salt as well.

It was the rare pioneer who wouldn't agree with the view that Bob Edwards was to express later in his Calgary Eye Opener, that the main difference between the Liberal and Conservative parties was that "one is in and the other is out".

And what settled the issue of who was in and who was out, as the following accounts of early Alberta elections show, was often a matter of down-to-earth practicality.

* * * *

IF HE WAS TO "RARE UP ON HIS HIND LAIGS . . ."

Long before Alberta became a province on its own, it was part of the North West Territory and, by 1885, Alberta settlers were about to be given their first chance to choose part of the new government.

Pioneer E. N. Barker describes the process:

"Of course it was not long after the province (NWT) began to settle up that elections came along, and ever after it has been stated that the air became warmer, and the summer frosts grew less, because of the amount of sultry atmosphere pipe in and out at the time of our numerous elections.

"The first election came along in 1885, not so very long after the Riel rebellion. This rebellion stirred up the east from a long and continuous slumber. Word came out onto the range that a member for the North West Assembly was to be elected . . .

"It was decided to run Lord Boyle, after the possibilities had been gone over. The real reason why His Lordship was chosen was that no one else knew anything about that sort of thing, and he, being a peer, was supposed to know something of parliamentary procedure.

"The canvassers who came out our way stated, 'He's the only man that can make a speech.'

"It seemed to be the general opinion that this was the great requisite, for, as one cow-puncher remarked, 'If we wuz to send a man down thar as our man, and he was to rare up on his hind laigs to say somethin' among them lawyers an' other fellers, an' he got himself rared up on his hind haunches an' dassen't say nothin' we'd look plumb foolish.' "

(As a matter of record, Lord Boyle was duly elected and, to the satisfaction of his constituents, he "rared up on his hind haunches" plumb good.)

* * * *

BREAD AND BUTTER VOTING . . .

One of the big problems in early Alberta elections, of course, was that so many of the settlers were too new to Canada to either understand what was happening or even much care.

We have a good example of this when, in 1891, the surprised pioneers of Cardston came up against their first federal election:

"One night," writes one of the Mormons, "we saw riding up the creek a bunch of horsemen who proved to be some Mounted Police, Arthur Harper, returning officer, and Jack Cowdray, the banker from Macleod, who was the scrutineer. Bob Giveen came along as scout and steerman.

"As soon as they stated their business, which was to hold an election, we cooked supper and put the whole bunch down on the floor to sleep.

"The next day, after breakfast, we all saddled up and rode over to the Ashe, Cotter and Derenzie Ranch to vote, for it was there that the poll was to be taken . . .

"A table was arranged in the house, at which sat the deputy returning officer and his poll clerk, and we stood up and said who we voted for. Whichever way a man voted, it must be known, as he had to announce in a loud voice who he voted for, so everyone around there knew and could go and tell about it.

"As Sir John MacDonald was in power, and D. W. Davis of Macleod was a Conservative, we four voters, all very young and not having had any previous experience in politics, concluded it was a waste of time trying to send one on the wrong side all the way down to Ottawa.

"So it was decided that as we all knew D.W. Davis, it would be better to vote for someone we knew and whom we could get at.

"Besides this, he was head of the I. G. Baker Co., at Macleod, and most of us dealt there, so that if we voted against him our credit in the future might be impaired. It was not considered good policy to go right against the firm that were the wholesale purveyors of this part of Alberta, were storekeepers, bankers et al for the whole of this section.

"We had been told that a man should not quarrel with his bread and butter, so of course D. W. Davis received a solid Conservative vote of four votes in the St. Mary's Polling Division."

* * * *

A MATTER OF TACTICS . . .

For a long time in Alberta, politics continued to be almost a game; one that called for quick wits and a little well-intentioned deception.

So, when the Hon. Arthur Sifton made a bid for re-election in the NWT council, he called for help on Paddy Nolan — the Irish-born Calgary lawyer with the quickest wits in Alberta.

It was quite a challenge for Nolan. Sifton's riding was in southern Alberta's mining country — which would have been all right but for one small point. Sifton had become an ardent prohibitionist. He wouldn't take a drink, nor would he buy one for another man.

As Nolan knew all too well, Sifton's attitude was going to cost him votes.

Nolan arrived in one of the key mining towns a few hours ahead of Sifton and gathered as many miners together as he could fit inside the town's principal bar.

After setting up a few rounds, he heaved a massive sigh and shook his head.

"Boys," he said gloomily, "you know Sifton is to speak here tonight. He's a fine fellow, but he has one failing that I fear may cost him many votes." He tapped his glass. "It's this," he said sadly. "Yes, this.

"You see, he's been dreaming about a night with the boys ever since the campaign started, but he doesn't know when to stop, and I have a devil of a time keeping him straight."

Suddenly an idea seemed to hit Nolan, and he brightened.

"Say, if you boys will help, I think we may just manage to pull him through this meeting! I want you to see that no one asks him to take a drink, for if anyone asks him he can't refuse — and if he takes even one drink, the Lord knows where he'll stop."

The miners, of course, were delighted to help old Paddy out, and the meeting that followed was one of Sifton's best — though he never found out exactly why.

* * * *

SALT RUNS OUT . . .

By 1905, Alberta had become a province in its own right; named for the Princess Louise Alberta by her husband the Marquis of Lorne.

Albertans were still taking their politics with a grain of salt, but the salt was running out. There was war in Europe, then a post-war economic sag that sagged right into the great depression.

By the 1920's, the people of Alberta were taking politics seriously indeed. And the traditional rivalry between Liberal and Conservative as to which was in and which was out was soon to be settled in the provincial arena.

Neither was going to be "in" in Alberta for a long time.

* * * *

ABERHART FOR ALBERTA . . .

The staying power of Alberta's Social Credit government is as spectacular as was its first landslide victory.

Boasting a longer life-span in office than any other democratically-elected government the world has known, the Socreds have held power for more than three and a half decades.

Behind it all was a big man with a Bible.

Portly, bald and bespectacled, William Aberhart became a high school principal when he arrived in Calgary in 1910.

It was a modest beginning for a man who would eventually mesmerize the population of the province.

Aberhart began his journey to political power along the straight and narrow road of religion. He taught Bible classes in Calgary churches for several years, then he organized a class of his own at Westbourne Baptist Church.

Few could guess that this class would become the nucleus of one of the most dynamic institutions in the province.

The Prophetic Bible Institute was founded in 1927 with William Aberhart as dean. Housed in a $65,000 building "with all modern conveniences" in the heart of Calgary, the PBI soon became the springboard for Aberhart's unparalleled evangelism.

His Sunday "Back to the Bible Hour" radio broadcasts captured the imagination of audiences nearing 350,000 people — half the entire population of the province.

* * * *

SOMETHING FOR EVERYONE . . .

Among those captivated by the radio broadcasts were the members of the fledgling Social Credit League, and soon league activities were revolving around the Bible institute and Aberhart its dynamic leader.

But Aberhart's message was not only spiritual. At a time when Alberta was writhing in the grips of depression, he came up with proposals for an economic cure-all.

He came upon his theories accidentally, while marking some examination papers in Edmonton in 1932. A friend had loaned him a book by British economist Major C.H. Douglas — the "founder of social credit". What Aberhart read in the book was to become the foundation of a political philosophy for Alberta.

At first, Bible Bill (as he was becoming widely known) tried to convince the members of the ruling United Farmers of Alberta party to adopt his ideas. But neither the UFA nor the traditional parties would have anything to do with this strange-sounding financial system.

So Aberhart returned to the pulpit and the airways to preach the message of social credit to the people.

Jobless and poverty-stricken, thousands of people heard him and took hope, while the business community reeled back with horror.

The social credit system, said Bible Bill, would provide a monthly "basic dividend" of $25 to every man, woman and child in the province.

The idea caught on like a prairie fire, and Alberta plunged into one of its bitterest election campaigns.

Not everyone, needless to say, was enthused by the possibility of a social credit government. Aberhart's single-mindedness had earned him powerful enemies in the whole political establishment of Alberta.

Conservative candidate Hugh C. Farthing (later an Alberta Supreme Court judge), for one, likened faith in social credit to "admitting to the world at large that we had got into our second childhood and still believed in Santa Claus."

But, on election day, Aug. 22, 1935, the Social Credit party swept 56 of the 63 seats in the Alberta legislature.

The overwhelming victory was, according to The Calgary Herald, "an uprising of a people demanding a new deal of some kind. It was a mass revolt against depression."

It was also an eloquent tribute to William Aberhart, the man whose booming voice and hell and brimstone speeches had penetrated to every corner of the province.

* * * *

PREDICAMENTS OF POWER . . .

Ironically, Aberhart was not a candidate in the 1935 election; it took a forced by-election to earn him a seat in the legislature, and his place as the new premier of Alberta.

But he had emerged triumphantly from the basement of the Bible Institute to take over the highest position in the province.

Before the election, Aberhart had swept aside all warnings about constitutional barriers to his radical reforms. But now the barriers seemed very real indeed.

Unable to fulfill an election pledge to establish social credit in Alberta within 18 months, Aberhart was even confronted with opposition from within his own party.

He managed to tame this, then went on to begin introducing his credit measures — the key to the total social security concept.

But the $25 dividends were not forthcoming.

One by one, Alberta's new government passed acts to control banks and bankers and the flow of credit. And, one by one, the federal government and the courts invalidated them.

The province was in an economic mire, but it is a tribute to the power of Aberhart that the people of Alberta never lost faith in him. His fiery personality and inexhaustible energy generated tremendous loyalty.

The economic boom that accompanied World War Two, and the major oil discoveries at Leduc finally turned the financial tide.

* * * *

THE VISION REMAINS . . .

Aberhart, right from the beginning, envisioned a brilliant future for Alberta. And he was convinced that this would be a future in which the Social Credit party played an unlimited role.

The vision was an accurate one. By 1970 the party had survived an unbroken string of nine elections.

And, when William Aberhart died in 1943, his carefully-groomed successor Ernest Manning carried the vision on — even succeeding Aberhart as the orator of the Back to the Bible Hour.

By the time Ernest Manning assumed power as premier, most of the far-fetched financial schemes of "Bible Bill" had faded into the past.

At least once in the Manning era, however, the Socreds found themselves doing battle with their time-honored enemy, the federal government. The Social Credit Bill of Rights, described by Manning as a new charter of freedom for Alberta, was declared unconstitutional by the Privy Council in 1946.

By 1964, with the economy booming, the Social Credit party had reached the heights Aberhart had dreamed of so many years before. It held 59 of the legislature's 63 seats, and a budget surplus of $50 million.

And today a third Social Credit premier, Harry Strom,

is in power and making the solid Socred promise of "a new era on a solid foundation".

The times have changed, the talk is calmer, but 36 years after the first Social Credit triumph there are still echoes of the evangelist premier who launched his party on its long journey through Alberta history.

* * * *

BEYOND POLITICS . . .

"Statesman" is a dangerous word to use in Alberta. There are too many people around who remember Bob Edwards' definition of a statesman as "a dead politician".

But, at the risk of raising Edwards' ghostly mirth, there are some Albertans who deserve the designation "statesman", in the finest sense of the word. R. B. Bennett, for example, who became Canada's prime minister. And Roland Michener, our present Governor-General.

There are many others, and there is one, in particular, for whom even Bob Edwards would willingly have suspended his definition.

* * * *

CANADA'S "INDIAN" SENATOR . . .

James Gladstone, in a way, is the personification of all the history of Alberta.

His memories go back to a childhood when he lived in a tee-pee on the open prairie, when transportation was a horse and a travois, and when the buffalo still ran free.

Now in his eighties, he talks with easy familiarity of men we associate with the very beginnings of our heritage — Col. Macleod, Jerry Potts, the famous Indian chiefs, a grandfather who built Fort Whoop-Up.

"All this was open country then," he muses in his home in Cardston. "Wherever we went we camped, and there was nothing to disturb us and no one to chase us away. All this land was ours. It belonged to us."

By "us", of course, James Gladstone means Alberta's Indian people. And that "us" is, at the same time, his favorite private joke and the greatest honor of his life.

"What Indian is in me," he explains with a twinkle of his blue eyes, "is from Winnipeg. That's where my grandfather married this girl — French half-breed as far as I can learn, according to the name of her and all. Best I can do is about an eighth Indian — by blood."

But "blood" isn't what counts with Jim Gladstone. By choice — and by appointment — he is an Indian, and the greatest statesman his people have.

Raised as an Indian boy, he spoke Cree before he spoke English, and was fluent in Blackfoot by the time he was 12.

From childhood on, he made it his destiny to fight for the rights of his people; a fight he still continues, and which paid off in the unique honor at age 33 of being legally adopted as a full treaty Indian by the Blackfoot.

He remembers that day as the greatest of his life. Greater even, perhaps, than the day in the 1950's when he heard that John Diefenbaker had appointed him a member of the Canadian Senate — the only "Indian" ever to be elevated to such high status in the dominion.

And if anyone ever wants to question just how Indian Jim Gladstone really is, all they have to do is look back to the day he made his maiden speech in Canada's upper house — in Blackfoot.

"You think Indians got a good deal in this country?" he

demands abruptly. "Well they haven't. And I'm not going to stop fighting till they do."

Jim Gladstone makes that a determined promise.

But, then, Jim Gladstone has all Alberta history within his life-span.

And, in the end, that kind of determination and promise may very well be what our Alberta heritage is all about. . . .